Adolescent Literacy and Differentiated Instruction

BARBARA KING-SHAVER AND ALYCE HUNTER

HEINEMANN

Portsmouth, NH

Heinemann
361 Hanover Street
Portsmouth, NH 03801–3912
www.heinemann.com

Offices and agents throughout the world

Library of Congress Cataloging-in-Publication Data
King-Shaver, Barbara.
   Adolescent literacy and differentiated instruction / Barbara King-Shaver and Alyce Hunter.
      p.   cm.
   Includes bibliographical references.
   ISBN-13: 978-0-325-02661-9
   ISBN-10: 0-325-02661-0
1. Language arts (Secondary).   2. Individualized instruction.   I. Hunter, Alyce.
II. Title.
   LB1631.K492 2009
   428.0071'2—dc22   2009012574

Editor: James Strickland
Production: Sonja S. Chapman
Typesetter: Cape Cod Compositors, Inc.
Cover design: Jenny Jensen Greenleaf
Manufacturing: Steve Bernier

Printed in the United States of America on acid-free paper
13 12 11 10 09   ML   1   2   3   4   5

To our professors at Douglass College,
who inspired us to appreciate each learner,
and to our fellow teachers, who continue to see
and believe in the potential of every student.

Contents

Foreword

By Carol Ann Tomlinson

When I reflect back on the early part of my career as a English teacher, I see the tall, angular young woman that was me, trying to master the previously unexplored terrain of bulletin board construction. I feel the Friday afternoon exhaustion that made me wonder if I could get from my classroom to my car at the end of the week. I recall (more than once) sitting up in bed after a dream that my students had taken over the classroom and I had no way to regain control of it.

I also recall with pristine clarity—almost as though I had watched the video yesterday—the moment at which fifteen-year-old Golden whispered to me in the hallway outside our seventh grade classroom that he could not read. And I hear Jonathan's impromptu definition of a symbol—preceded by a sigh that no-doubt indicated he was ready to move on, even if the rest of us weren't. "A symbol," eleven-year-old Jonathan told us as he exhaled, "is a concrete representation of an abstract entity."

By the time I met Golden and Jonathan, I was a third year teacher. In August, I felt for the first time like I was a "real" teacher. The students had not eaten me for lunch—nor appropriated control of the classroom. I had cool bulletin boards. AND, I had a curriculum notebook for my grade and subject, given to me by the school in which I was about to start teaching.

It turns out that all three indicators of having reached some secure state of professionalism were illusory. In time, I came to see bulletin boards were more cleverness than substance. I began to understand that I needed to aspire to be a leader of my students rather than to be in control of them. And having Golden and Jonathan in the same class led me to the disorienting epiphany that even a curriculum that doesn't fit the kids for whom it was designed is little better than a theory that fails to address the dilemma with which it is paired.

I suppose that teaching involves a healthy dose of on-the-job-training. In my case, I am astounded, however, at how many solutions I needed to invent—and how often I felt alone in trying to craft a way to address a student or classroom need. I didn't know how to teach reading—and yet Golden trusted me with his secret and I couldn't let him down. I had no idea what to do with Jonathan, who knew more about everything than I did.

I didn't know how to think about our curriculum in a way that helped me plan for both Jonathan and Golden (and the other 150 students who came through my door daily). I didn't know how to honor the potential of each of my students and to knit us into a team that worked to help everyone succeed. I didn't know how to arrange time so that everyone got some of me in some configuration smaller than the-class-as-a-whole. I had a woefully small toolkit of instructional strategies. I didn't know how to help my students (or their parents) understand why we needed a classroom that deviated from the face-the-front-and-move-along-together rules that were clearly older and more venerated than I was.

Persistently and over time, I invented what I now call "differentiated instruction." (I don't recall the way I taught having a name during the 21 years I was in a public school classroom. It was just how things needed to be in order to work for the distinctly unmatched set of students that came to me each year.) I learned a number of ways to help young adolescents read—and to want to read. I learned about what high-end challenge meant—and didn't mean. I figured out how to talk with students and their parents about a classroom designed to elicit the best from each of its members—and to give each student my best efforts.

I invented the Gram-ball board and super sentences and learning contracts and tiering and a way to handle spelling and vocabulary in classes where student reading readiness inevitably stretched from first grade to college level. I figured out ways to help disorganized kids string coherent thoughts together on paper. I figured out how to manage time and space and (scant) resources flexibly.

Mind you, I'm not saying I was the first person, or the only one, to invent those strategies or to craft similar solutions to those classroom issues. What I'm saying is that I was so alone in what I was trying to do that if anyone had similar or better ideas, I simply didn't know about them.

All of this flashback to my journey as a teacher—and more than a little nostalgia for the public school classroom—resulted from my reading of Barbara King-Shaver and Alyce Hunter's manuscript. It would have been a gift of considerable magnitude if it had been available to me in the years I spent in solitary invention.

In truth, of course, I learned a lot by creating answers that suited my setting, and I wouldn't have lasted as a teacher if someone had forced me to use a scripted text or a pacing straight-jacket. Nonetheless, it would have saved me a great deal of time and given me a sense of partnership had *Adolescent Literacy and Differentiated Instruction* been in my line of vision.

The authors understand the classroom as a system with interrelated parts. They don't peddle strategies devoid of curriculum. They don't underplay the critical role assessment plays in informing instruction. They don't neglect the critical need for learning to be joyful for students. They understand the imperative of addressing student readiness, interest, and learning profile in the secondary grades. They don't assume that teaching reading is only for elementary classrooms and for secondary resource rooms. Their work with literacy and with differentiation is rooted in solid scholarship. Quite simply, I would love to have had this resource as a secondary language arts teacher—both when I taught in high school and in middle school. I'd have happily implemented their ideas about persuasive writing stations, revision stations, station rotations, prewriting, and revision choice boards to my repertoire. My students and I would have been their beneficiaries.

The book also makes me itch to go back to my secondary classroom to see how I could use contemporary technologies as vehicles for differentiation. Podcasts, wikis, blogs, digital books, video book trailers, multi modal choice boards, graphic novels, digital portfolios, and the web offer limitless possibilities to connect the full range of contemporary learners with the skills, ideas, issues, and possibilities that propel their world. With their application of these strategies to the secondary language arts classroom, they help us access Differentiation 2.0.

I'm grateful to be able to learn from this book and its authors. They would have made me a better educator when my career began. They will make me a better educator now. I hope that will be the case for many other educators of adolescents as well.

Acknowledgments

We could not have written this book without the help of those teachers who willingly shared their lessons and experiences with us. We are especially thankful for our colleagues at West Morris Regional High School District in Chester, New Jersey, and at South Brunswick High School in Monmouth Junction, New Jersey. Thank you.

We could not have written this book without the help of our editor and friend Jim Strickland and the supportive staff at Heinemann. Thank you.

We could not have written this book without the support and thoughtfulness of our spouses, Phil Shaver and Bob Hunter, and our children and their spouses, Jay, Sean, Scott, Alyson, Jessica, Kari, Dawn, Lisa, Joseph, and Brian and Michele and Gavin. Finally, we could not have written this book without the inspiration and perspective provided by our grandchildren, Robin and Will and Luke, Alton, Jay, Brooke, and Lorelai. Thank you.

Introduction

Our first book, *Differentiated Instruction in the English Classroom: Content, Process, Product, and Assessment* (2003), was written as a primer to help other educators understand the basics of differentiated instruction. It provided clear examples of various strategies used by real teachers as they experimented with determining students' readiness, interests, and different learning styles. We wrote the book as a labor of love to address all of those students we had taught over our more than fifty combined years of teaching. We wrote the book, too, as a labor of collaboration to speak to all of those teachers like us who struggled to meet the needs of that one special learner and all of those spectacular learners. The book, in its fifth printing, has become the basis for numerous staff development workshops, including a Pre-AP workshop. In addition, many young teachers tell us they were assigned the text in an education course, and they are now applying the content in their own classrooms.

So it seems that we needed to continue our journey, our writing, and our collaboration to address some of the additional concerns and challenges faced by English language arts teachers in 2010 and beyond. Our focus continues to be on differentiated instruction, as it is our belief that differentiation is the way to educate each student. This focus on differentiated instruction is combined with a realization that today's adolescent faces unique challenges as a reader, writer, speaker, viewer, thinker, and learner. Because knowledge and access to knowledge are exploding at a phenomenal rate, today's adolescents are faced with making sense of a world that is forever changing. As our editor, Jim Strickland, and his wife, Kathleen, remind us in their book *Engaged in Learning: Teaching English, 6–12* (2002), it is the responsibility of all teachers to provide students with opportunities to develop. Therefore, considering the changing world of adolescents, and in view of our obligation to help these adolescents develop, along with the expansion and proliferation of concepts relating to differentiated instruction, we decided to undertake the writing of this new book.

We wrote this book to celebrate again the differences that are presented by adolescent learners. We wrote this book to address anew the ways to differentiate what we do in instruction and in the materials we select to teach adolescents reading, writing, speaking, listening, viewing, and the new literacies. We wrote this book to consider new ways of assessing how we know what students know, how they know what they know, and how they become responsible for what they know. Finally, this book was written to unite the myriad of teachers like ourselves who see differentiated instruction as an essential way to teach and to learn.

The first two chapters in this book address the relationship of adolescent literacy and differentiated instruction and provide planning models for differentiating instruction for adolescent literacy. The third chapter includes a discussion of assessment, focusing on both formative and summative assessments. Chapters 4 to 8 address how differentiated instruction can be used to support specific literacies: reading, writing, speaking and listening, and viewing. The viewing chapter, Chapter 6, also includes multimedia examples. Chapter 8 is devoted to the new digital literacies of the twenty-first century. The final chapter looks at literacy beyond the English language arts classroom. Although the sample lessons and differentiated tasks presented in this book were created for the English language arts classroom, the strategies on which they are based apply to all content areas across the curriculum. Finally, a glossary is included to clarify both general and specific terms related to differentiated instruction.

Also please note that while every effort has been made to provide accurate Internet addresses, we (neither the authors nor the publisher) do not assume any responsibility for changes that occur after publication.

Adolescent Literacy and Differentiated Instruction

What is adolescent literacy? Researchers and educators continue to define and debate the definition of adolescent literacy. For many years, the term *literacy* was applied primarily to elementary students learning to read and write. Recently, however, educators and policy makers have turned their attention to adolescent learners. Research reports and other publications on adolescent literacy provide three different interpretations of the term. Some sources focus only on reading when they refer to adolescent literacy; some, however, broaden the definition of literacy: "Literacy and reading, though related, are neither synonymous nor ambiguous, terms. Typically reading is subsumed by literacy, with the latter term used to refer to reading, writing, and other modes of symbolic communication" (Alverman 2001, 4).

This book supports the expanded description of adolescent literacy offered by The National Council of Teachers of English (NCTE) in its policy research brief on this topic:

> Literacy encompasses reading, writing and a variety of social and intellectual practices that call upon the voice as well as the eye and hand. It also

extends to the new media—including non-digitalized multimedia, digitalized multimedia, hypertext or hypermedia. (NCTE 2006, 16)

Adolescent literacy, in the broadest sense, can be defined as the way teenagers make sense of their world. It is how they literally and figuratively use the tools of education combined with what they learn and know from outside the classroom to comprehend and understand the today and, more importantly, the tomorrow of their lives. It includes such diverse yet inclusive skills as being literate in reading, writing, speaking, listening, viewing, and technology. It also includes the facility to learn and be able to explain concepts from various content areas, such as mathematics, social studies, and science.

The aspect that unites all of these apparent divergent literacies is the ability of adolescent learners to be self-directed and reflective about their own learning. Specifically, "A Call for Action: What We Know About Adolescent Literacy and Ways to Support Teachers in Meeting Students' Needs" (NCTE 2004) encourages teachers to help adolescents view text broadly as print, electronic, and visual media. Students should be encouraged to think critically as they engage with such text and also to examine how and what these texts are saying and implying. Furthermore, this call to action propels teachers to create an environment where students engage in making meaning by analyzing, deconstructing, and reconstructing these texts. Such an environment is a classroom where differentiated instruction is the norm. Differentiated instruction honors every learner's pursuit of literacy through the teacher's diagnosing and acting upon the learner's readiness, interests, and learning style. The teacher creates an inclusive environment through the celebration of diverse avenues to learn content, apply process, produce a product, and grow through assessment.

The Need to Address Adolescent Literacy

Recent reports, such as those from the National Assessment of Educational Progress (NAEP 2007) and American College Testing (ACT 2006), have identified what an NCTE report calls an "under-literate class of adolescents" (NCTE 2006). According to recent data, nearly half of high school graduates lack the reading skills needed to pass first-year college courses (ACT 2006), and only 59 percent of the students tested were deemed ready for college work. However, the overall scores for English showed a slight (2 percent) increase in 2006 over 2004. These results are reported at a time when the growth of a global community demands a more literate workforce. The NAEP assessment program reported mixed results in 2007. Reading scores for eighth graders increased, while scores for twelfth graders showed an overall decline in reading compared to the 1992 scores. The average writing scores for both eighth and twelfth graders increased slightly over 1992. The concern of educators and policy makers is that high school graduates in this country will not be ready to compete in a demanding, rapidly changing world. The concern for adolescent literacy is so great that the International Reading Association identified it as a "hot topic" for both 2007 and 2008. Adolescent learners face many new literacy demands as they move into middle school and high school. In the elementary grades, most reading is of works of fiction. At the middle and secondary levels, students are required to read more challenging texts, including more sophisticated literature and more expository texts, such as textbooks and essays. These texts present new challenges to the adolescent reader. Yet, few adolescents receive ongoing literacy instruction. In the middle and secondary grades, students are also asked to compose increasingly sophisticated pieces of writing for different purposes and audiences. Teachers now recognize that adolescents benefit from literacy instruction throughout the high school years, yet not all adolescents need the same amount or type of literacy instruction and support. In addition, teachers also recognize that they need to broaden the definition of literacy to include not only the traditional skills of reading, writing, speaking, listening, and viewing, but also the new multimedia and digital literacies.

In a high school classroom, the range of learners is vast. The challenge for the classroom teacher is how to address the range of needs these diverse learners present. Douglas B. Fisher of San Diego State University acknowledges the problem of adolescent literacy, and he suggests that "with the diverse student needs seen today, it is time for less prescriptive and more 'personal' teaching differentiated for each student" (2007, 12). Adolescent learners can benefit from individualized, differentiated learning plans. Educators need to ensure that students receive instruction at the appropriate level. In addition, as a recent NCTE research report reminds teachers, "When instruction does not address adolescent's literacy needs, motivation and engagement are diminished" (NCTE 2006, 5).

In "Adolescent Literacy: A Policy Research Brief" (NCTE 2007), six key practices that promote adolescent literacy through research-based teaching practices are highlighted:

1. Demystify content-specific literacy practice.

2. Motivate through meaningful choice.

3. Engage students with real-world literacy practice.

4. Affirm multiple literacy.

5. Support learner-centered environment.

6. Foster social responsibility through multicultural literacy.

Because differentiated classrooms are student-centered, taking students from their individual entry points into the curriculum and moving them toward common goals, differentiated instruction provides a way for classroom teachers to address each of these six points.

The first factor identified in the NCTE Research Brief is to demystify content-specific literacy practices by having English teachers work collaboratively with their colleagues in other disciplines to develop instructional strategies in literacy that can be used across the curriculum to help students learn any subject matter better. As the NCTE report notes, middle and high school teachers need to "show students how literacy operates within the academic disciplines" so that adolescents can "learn from the texts they read" (NCTE 2007). This includes language across the curriculum strategies that address the differentiated needs of adolescent learners.

Choice, the second key practice identified, is a major factor in motivating adolescents to learn, and it is a major component of differentiated instruction in all disciplines. Building choice into an assignment provides a way to address student differences in academic readiness, personal interests, and learning styles. Strategies that support differentiated instruction, such as tic-tac-toe, tiered assignments, and learning stations, can be structured to incorporate an element of choice.

The third key factor identified in the NCTE report, real-world practices, provides another opportunity for differentiating instruction. When assignments are constructed to reflect literacy practices outside the classroom, different purposes and text forms offer a practical way to differentiate tasks. For example, when reading and producing persuasive texts, some students may identify a company they wish to correspond with about a product they used, and others may decide to write a letter to the editor about rules for skateboarding in their town. Still other students may write in a blog on censorship and the movies.

The fourth factor, affirming multiple literacies, is built into many differentiated instruction strategies. Tic-tac-toe or choice boards, for example, can offer students choices among an array of multimodal assignments. These can incorporate Howard Gardner's multiple intelligences (1983) or offer print as well as digital choices. Because differentiated instruction is built on the premise that students learn in different ways, differentiated learning activities embrace multiple literacies.

The fifth key practice identified in the NCTE Research Brief (2007) is supporting a learner-centered environment. Differentiated classrooms use a variety of methods for presenting, processing, and assessing learning. The practices teachers use—individual, group, and whole-class instruction—are based on demonstrated need. Ongoing assessments help the teacher identify what instruction individual students need at different times during a unit of study. The goal in a differentiated classroom is for the students to receive the type and amount of instruction they need in order to reach the identified goals and to become independent learners.

The final key factor identified in the NCTE report is fostering social responsibility through multicultural literacy. Differentiated practices offer opportunities for adolescents to reach beyond their local communities. Reading multicultural literature and communicating with diverse audiences through the Internet are two ways teachers can make adolescents aware of their responsibilities as members of a multicultural community. Building on student interests, teachers can design assignments that reach beyond the classroom.

Differentiated instruction helps teachers focus on the needs of adolescent literacy learners. It allows the teacher to build lessons based on student strengths and to provide instruction for student weaknesses. As Carol Ann Tomlinson notes, differentiated instruction "is about making sure the learning fits the learner" (2008, 28). Adolescent learners need and deserve English language arts teachers who know how to assess what these learners know and are able to do. Such enlightened educators, after assessment, can plan and teach literacy support strategies to help each student. Irvin, Meltzer, and Dukes (2007) define these strategies as instructional methods and activities that support learning by "breaking down" literacy into smaller, more manageable "chunks." For some students, these chunks could include using a graphic organizer to outline and connect nonfiction text. For others, these chunks could mean participating in a Socratic seminar to think collaboratively about a reading selection. The teacher's goal in using such differentiated literacy support strategies is to help every learner become more independent. Irvin, Meltzer, and Dukes (2007) further challenge English language arts educators to consider that there are really only two main tasks with regard to all of literacy teaching and learning. Instructors must match students' needs, interest, and learning styles not only to instruction but also to appropriate text. Therefore, the English language arts educator must be knowledgeable about ways to differentiate instruction and select materials to support success and independence.

Adolescent Literacy and Planning for Differentiated Instruction

2

Differentiated instruction is difficult to define simply. Differentiated instruction is a philosophy about teaching and learning. According to Carol Ann Tomlinson (1999, 2003), a pioneer in the field, differentiated instruction requires teachers to look at their students, not just at what they teach. The goal of differentiated instruction is to take each learner from his or her entry point into the curriculum and move him or her forward in learning. But differentiated instruction is not just about academic achievement. Differentiation "helps students not only master content, but also form their own identities as learners" (Tomlinson 2008, 26).

Differentiating instruction is a process in which teachers look at students and their achievements through multiple lenses. First, teachers act as diagnosticians to examine and determine students' needs, abilities, readiness, experiences, interests, and learning styles. Inventories, vocabulary work, and focused discussions are some of the ways English language arts teachers learn about their classes and the needs of individuals. Teachers then determine how to differentiate instruction. They need to consider multiple ways to present content, process, and product. They need to decide the answers to these questions and other questions to help them differentiate instruction. What standards should be used to judge which content should be learned by all? What content should be selected to challenge learners? How can the process of reading—including prereading, during-reading, and postreading strategies—be incorporated into middle and high school English language arts classes so that the needs of superior and struggling readers can be met? How can the writing process be individualized to challenge those who can write expository essays to refine their work and to assist those who still have difficulty with organization and mechanics? How can teachers determine what product will best exemplify and celebrate student achievement? Will writing a paper, giving a presentation, or taking a pencil-and-paper test be best? What material—books, short stories, media, technology—can be used? How will teachers assess that learners have learned what is required and assigned?

Concerns of Middle and High School Teachers About Differentiated Instruction

English language arts teachers have numerous concerns about how they can accomplish differentiated content, process, and product as they consider student readiness, interests, and learning styles. In *Differentiated Instruction in the English Classroom: Content, Process, Product, and Assessment* (2003), we counsel teachers to consider even homogeneously grouped classrooms as diverse and ripe for differentiation success. We tell English language arts instructors that it is not necessary to differentiate every day for all students. Also, advice is given on how to arrange a classroom for flexible grouping and how to manage student behavior. Additionally, Nunley (2006) identifies and then debunks other obstacles that high school teachers believe inhibit their ability to differentiate instruction. One obstacle frequently identified is that high school educators have too much content to cover due to the pressures of state graduation testing and standardized testing, such as the Scholastic Achievement Test (SAT) and the American College Test (ACT). Nunley recommends that teachers "cover" basic content in formats they are familiar with, such as lecturing, and then allow students choice as to how to process and "play" with the information. Nunley (2006) also addresses another comment frequently made by high school educators: that differentiated instruction is for elementary schools. Teachers are reminded that such techniques and strategies work for all learners. Some high school students have difficulty reading and could be permitted to use technology and new literacy strategies, such as visuals, to help them understand content and develop process. Most importantly, this author reminds teachers that they are not alone in their quest to improve instruction and student performance. Nunley instructs high school teachers to consult and work with teaching peers to learn and reinforce knowledge of and practice with differentiated instruction.

Finally, the National Association of Secondary School Principals, in its comprehensive guide *Creating a Culture of Literacy: A Guide for Middle and High School Principals* (2005), urges not only teachers but also secondary school administrators to be cognizant of the different and diverse literacy needs of today's diverse high school students. Middle school and high school educators are reminded that even though historically literacy instruction has not been thought of as a secondary school issue, it is today. Students' background knowledge and readiness need to be acknowledged. Teachers need to be highly trained to plan and deliver instruction that includes strategies to accelerate invention, like the strategies that are earmarked in differentiated instruction.

Planning for Differentiated Instruction

Once English language arts teachers at the middle school or high school levels decide that differentiation is something they would like to try or need to do, they should consider how to plan successfully. Tomlinson and McTighe (2006) contend that differentiated instruction and the universally common planning tools of Understanding by Design (UBD) are not only compatible but, more importantly, are necessary to each other. They distinguish between the two ideas by stating that the UBD model focuses primarily on the "what" and "how" teachers teach. Differentiated instruction also focuses on the "how" but emphasizes the "whom" and "where" of teaching. The UBD design stresses that the circumstances for altering the established goals, understandings, and essential questions of the framework are limited. Sometimes students' Individualized Education Plans or their advanced knowledge may cause teachers to alter these common components. However, most curriculum planning should acknowledge the same goals, understandings, and essential questions for all learners. Differentiation may be necessary for the assessment evidence section of the model, where teachers need to use what they know about students' interests, readiness, and learning styles to possibly alter performance tasks, other evidence, and key criteria. The final section of the model, the Education Plan, should be flexible and differentiated to meet the needs of different students.

Bender (2008) suggests that differentiation is the ideal support for special education, inclusive education, and regular education teachers to practice the tenets of the popular special education concept of universal design. Universal design challenges all teachers to remove barriers, literally and figuratively, for students with disabilities. It asks teachers to design and implement classrooms, activities, lessons, curricula, and assessments that are flexible, simple, and equitable. It also asks that teachers provide students with choice to increase their ownership of and responsibility for learning. Lessons should be structured with clear directions, frequent breaks, and peer or partner clarification. Bender urges teachers to tier activities, a practice common to differentiated instruction, as a way to address common curricular goals for all students. Additionally, differentiated assessments can be a way to verify and celebrate the accomplishments of students.

Our first book on differentiation (2003) included differentiated lessons based on the works of Shakespeare, Miller, McBride, and others. These lessons were planned and organized using a basic planning guide that we proposed and devised to be used to direct teachers' thinking and lesson preparation. This planning guide is included as Figure 2–1. Teachers are asked to consider modes of differentiation in the contexts of unit planning, essential questions, strategies, and assignments.

Educators should not think of this guide as a lockstep, linear planner in which they must begin with unit and essential questions. Rather, this guide should be used as part of the writing process to compose lessons. It should be used in a recursive manner in which the users rewrite, clarify, and experiment before they complete lesson plans. For example, a number of the teachers in the West Morris

Figure 2–1

Persuasive Writing Planning Guide

Course Title and Level: Grade 10 English

Unit: Persuasive Writing

Essential Questions

How do we persuade someone else to accept our opinions?

How can writing be used as a method of persuasion?

Unit-Specific Questions

How does the purpose affect what we write?

How does the audience affect what we write?

What strategies can a writer use to persuade an audience?

Knowledge/Skills

format for a persuasive essay

persuasive devices

Modes of Differentiation Used

Content:

differentiate topic by choice

differentiate audience by choice

Process:

differentiate time frame

differentiate conferences

Based on (readiness, interests, learning styles)

interests

readiness

Strategies: tiered tasks, choice boards, stations

Regional High School District (New Jersey) decided that they wanted to use the choice board strategy as a way to enhance their students' ownership of the works they were reading. So they selected this strategy first and then determined why and how to differentiate.

A lesson plan format to expand and flesh out this basic planning guide is presented in Figure 2–2. This model is used more as a daily lesson plan rather than a unit plan. The column on the left lists the components of all lessons. The middle column contains whole-class activities, and the final column shows detailed differentiated activities. This particular lesson plan uses the lesson goal or purpose of identifying persuasive devices, a literacy skill that challenges secondary students to look deeply into a text to analyze how a writer affects the audience.

Planning for differentiated instruction requires that teachers know their students as individuals whose readiness, interests, and learning styles are important to their learning. It also requires that teachers have considerable knowledge about instructional methods and materials as they choose content, processes, products, and assessments to match their students' literacy strengths and needs. Planning and instruction need to place every student at the heart of experiences in reading, writing, speaking, listening, viewing, and the new literacies. Teachers need to consider how they assess what students already know, what students are learning, and how proficient they are in displaying what they understand.

Figure 2–2

Teacher Lesson Planning Guide

Unit: Persuasive Day One

Lesson Goal(s): Identifying persuasive devices used in writing

	Whole-Class Activity	Differentiated Strategy
"Do now" or sponge activity	Preassessment: Students complete a terminology list on persuasive devices, identifying those they know. Teacher does a quick check on their understanding.	Based on the students' previous performances and using the feedback obtained from the terminology list, the teacher assigns the groups.
Introduction	Students read their copies silently as the teacher reads aloud an editorial from a newspaper.	Advanced level: Students read the two opposing views on the *USA Today* editorial page. They then make a list comparing the persuasive devices used in each. Next, students evaluate which editorial they find most persuasive and explain why.
Core lesson	Class discussion in which the students identify different persuasive devices used in the editorial. Working in small, teacher-assigned groups, students read another editorial, then identify and label the devices the author used to persuade the audience.	Basic level: The teacher works with this group at the beginning of the activity to clarify any misunderstandings and to provide more examples of each type of persuasive device.
Closing activity	Students complete exit slips addressing one thing they learned today and one question they still have about persuasive devices.	If a student did not learn anything new, that student can write two questions he or she has about how best to persuade a reader or identify which persuasive device he feels is most successful and why.

Assessment and Differentiated Instruction

A s educators' view of teaching and learning changed during the past decade, so too did their view of assessment. Assessment is no longer viewed only as a test given by the teacher to the whole class at the end of a unit; assessment is now seen as an integral part of the whole learning process. Assessment today can be a group discussion, an individual teacher-student conference, or a digital presentation. But the medium for presenting evidence of learning is only one way in which assessment has changed. Teachers now recognize that assessment takes place during a unit as well as at its end. They recognize that students can take a more active role in the assessment process. And they recognize that students may demonstrate their learning in different ways.

Assessment needs to be aligned with instruction. This alignment begins during the planning stage when a teacher identifies the goals for the unit that clearly present what every student should know and be able to do at the end of the unit and what key concepts and skills students need to understand in order to be proficient. In a differentiated classroom, the goals remain the same, but the instruction that students receive and the assessments they complete may differ based on their readiness levels, interests, and learning styles. Because the goals remain the same, the teacher needs checkpoints along the way to identify which students need differentiated help to reach those goals. The first part of this chapter focuses on academic readiness. Assessment of interests and learning styles is discussed in the latter half of this chapter.

Preassessment for Academic Readiness

Once the goals for a unit are clearly identified, the next step in differentiating instruction is preassessment. Until teachers ascertain where their students are currently performing in relationship to the unit goals, teachers do not know when or how to differentiate instruction. Students need to be measured against a clearly identified standard or goal. Preassessments may be formal or informal. In a literacy classroom, the preassessments may take the form of a writing sample or a prereading vocabulary checklist. Teacher observations and reports on prior performance are also helpful when preassessing students' levels of readiness. Once this information is obtained, differentiated lessons and tasks can be presented based on student needs. Preassessment is actually the first component of ongoing, formative assessment.

Formative and Summative Assessment

During the assessment debates over the past twenty years, educators have become familiar with identifying assessment methods as summative or formative. Summative assessment evidence is gathered at the end of a unit of study or course. The data obtained from summative assessments may be used for many purposes: to report a grade, to make a student placement, to evaluate a program. In the classroom, summative assessment data may be used to help the teacher change what will be taught or how it will be taught next time. Formative assessments, on the other hand, are ongoing assessments that occur during a unit of study and are used for very different purposes. Formative assessments help teachers and students during the learning process, not at the end of it. Formative assessments are not graded. The evidence obtained from formative assessments is used to identify what has been learned in respect to given goals and what has not yet been mastered. Based on the evidence obtained from formative assessments, teachers provide additional or new instruction. Assessment helps each student move toward proficiency by providing feedback while the student is learning.

In his book expounding the transformative nature of formative assessment, James Popham (2008) emphasizes the roles of teachers and students in formative assessment. Popham argues that during formative assessments, teachers make adjustments in instruction and students make adjustments in their learning tactics. Teachers adjust their instructional activities, and students adjust the strategies they are using to learn. For example, Popham tells of the student who revises quickly after writing her essays, noting that she may need to change her tactics by letting the paper "cool off" between drafts before revising. Because not all students use the same learning strategies, the instruction they receive and the suggestions for how to improve need to be differentiated. Formative assessment and differentiated instruction are a natural fit. Once the formative assessment evidence is obtained during the ongoing learning process, the teacher can identify those students who need additional instruction and create tasks that will help them master the content. The evidence collected during formative assessments is key to helping teachers plan differentiated tasks.

The importance of formative assessment cannot be overstated. As Grant Wiggins (2006) points out, "The more you teach without finding out who understands the information and who doesn't, the greater the likelihood that only already proficient students will succeed" (1). Formative assessment drives instruction. It shows the teacher what is working and what is not. It shows the teacher which students understand and can apply the learning and which cannot.

Formative Assessment and Grading

Because the purpose of formative assessment is to provide feedback for the student and teacher so that the student can learn better, many educators agree that it should not be graded. Popham (2008) notes that "none of the assessments functioning as part of the formative assessment process ought to be graded. The function of formative assessment's evidence gathering is to help teachers and students make decisions intended to enhance students' learning. Therefore, teachers should build and use assessments to gather evidence of what it is students know and can do not to compare students' performances" (7). Rick Wormeli (2006b) agrees with Popham and reminds us that "in differentiated classes, grading focuses on clear and consistent evidence of mastery, not on the medium through which students demonstrate that mastery." He adds, "Of course if the test format is the assessment we do not allow students to opt for something else" (130). Wormeli explains that although not grading formative assessments is the ideal, there may be times when, in order to motivate some students, a teacher needs to give points for work completed. Rather than grade the work, formative assessments should be used to provide feedback to the teacher and the student.

Feedback

The reason formative assessment is so helpful is that it provides feedback early on, during the learning process. The more often students receive feedback before they are evaluated, the better their chances of achieving the goals. The most useful feedback not only tells the students how they are doing based on established goals or criteria but also what they need to do in order to reach those goals. They need assessment with guidance. Popham (2008) refers to this as "descriptive feedback," which can be applied to both the product and the process. Susan Brookhart (2008) notes that feedback can also be a motivational factor. When students understand what they must do to improve, they feel they have more control over their own learning and are motivated to continue working on the assignments.

Teachers of writing recognized early on that putting a grade and comments on a paper after it was written did little to improve their students' writing. Students just looked at the grade and filed the papers away, rarely paying any attention to the comments. The writing conference model was developed out of the need to give feedback during the process, when students could apply the advice they were given to the written product they were producing.

This model can be applied to other aspects of the literacy as well. For example, teachers can meet with students who are reading literature to discuss their understanding of the text as well as answer any questions they have. Feedback is also important for addressing any concerns about the reading process. This is especially helpful for those students who have difficulty reading challenging texts. Talking to them about the strategies they use during the reading process will help them apply previously learned literacy skills to new texts.

Teachers often use flexible grouping in a differentiated classroom. Groups, as well as individuals, need feedback on both process and products. Teachers can visit groups as they are working and provide feedback as students discuss novels or plan projects. Although this method of providing feedback is not new in the English language arts classroom, the configuration of the groups may be. Because students may be grouped based on interests, readiness levels, or learning styles, the feedback given to each group may be differentiated. Students who are grouped according to readiness levels often have different questions about their reading. It is not uncommon for advanced readers to be discussing recurring motifs and basic readers to be focusing on plot. Students who are grouped according to interest levels for a project will need to be referred to different resources. Students who are grouped according to learning styles may need different resources and different spaces.

Differentiation and Feedback

One of the main challenges for teachers is having enough time to give feedback to every student. Obviously, this is not possible for every assignment. Teachers need to decide which assignments are key to the learning of new concepts and skills and focus on those for differentiating assessment, including feedback. In addition, based on previous performance, teachers can identify those students who need more immediate feedback and meet with them individually or in small groups. Small-group meetings work when the teacher identifies a common problem. When the classroom is set up for differentiated practices, teachers can meet with individuals or small groups while their classmates are engaged in established practices such as completing tic-tac-toe boards or working on anchor activities. Feedback can also be built into a station activity, with one of the stations requiring some students to meet with the teacher.

When there is not time to provide oral feedback to all students who need it, teachers can provide written observations and suggestions. They do this by collecting works in progress and returning them with attached comments. These comments should not contain grades. As noted earlier, once students see grades on their work, they are less likely to revise or continue working.

Another way to differentiate feedback is to ask students what help they need. This becomes more effective as the year progresses. Students can be shown how to self-assess. They can be asked to write down questions they have about what they are studying. For example, a student was confused when he encountered the dialect in Hurston's *Their Eyes Were Watching God* (1999) and had stopped reading, but because his teacher asked the class to write down questions and submit them as exit slips when they left the room, she was able to meet the next day with the boy who had a problem and show him how to approach the dialect in the book. Her use of feedback helped the student before he fell too far behind in his reading of the novel.

A helpful hint about feedback is to "get the *but* out"—avoid the word *but* when giving feedback. Instead of saying, "I like your introduction, but it is missing a transition into the next paragraph," a teacher could say, "I like your introduction, and next we are going to look at how to make the transition into the next paragraph better." When students hear *but*, they tend to forget everything that was said previously and focus only on the negative comments that follow. Students are more willing to redo work and continue to learn when descriptive feedback is presented in a positive way.

Rubrics

Most English language arts teachers are now familiar with rubrics, scoring guides that contain criteria for achieving a specified point value for a completed product. Giving rubrics to students before they complete an assignment is key to providing useful feedback. When a rubric will be used for the final evaluation of the work, students need to know this. They need to know what the requirements for good work are and how they will be judged. Rubrics can be used during the learning process to give specific feedback on how students measure up to the criteria. Teachers can use rubrics to give feedback during the process, and students can self-assess using them.

Teachers have used rubrics as a way to differentiate instruction by assigning different point values to different parts of the rubric. For example, if it has been determined that a student needs to pay more attention to writing mechanics, then this part of the rubric could be weighted more than other sections on organization and fluency. Eventually, the student could be asked prior to an assignment how to weight different parts of the rubric. This would reinforce that the student is in control and responsible for his or her own learning. Sometimes teachers ask a learner to reflect during the process of an assignment whether the point values originally assigned remain valid and to explain why the values should be changed or remain the same. The learner also could be asked when the assignment is finished to reexamine the points originally assigned to determine whether these values helped in the learning process.

Another way that teachers have used rubrics to differentiate instruction and encourage learners to be responsible for their individual success, is to use "yes-no" checklists that ask students to make a yes or no determination in answering questions about the work. Teachers can further differentiate assessment by using both traditional and yes-no rubrics for the same assignment but adjusting the rubric type according to student's ability and needs.

Whether a teacher uses oral or written comments or rubrics, it is important that the feedback is tailored to the needs of the students, is presented during the formative assessment process, and is as descriptive as possible.

Differentiated Academic Assessments and Fairness

When using different assessment tools, the question of "fairness" always comes up. Wormeli (2006a) reminds us that "fair isn't always equal" (23), explaining that *fair* does not mean *the same*. What is fair for a student is doing what that student needs in order to continue to learn and grow; therefore, students in a class may be doing different work with different assessments as they strive to reach a common goal. Teachers need to be careful to separate the demonstration of understanding from the medium used to present it. It would be unfair, for example, to force a student to demonstrate his learning by speaking in front of a class if that student has a problem with speaking in front of large groups.

Assessment for Interests and Learning Styles

Students learn better when they are interested in and feel personally connected to the subject matter. Knowing a student's likes and dislikes, hobbies and pastimes can help the teacher differentiate lessons and tasks based on interests. In addition, students are more likely to complete assignments and pursue topics in depth when the material is presented in a way that addresses their personal learning preferences or learning styles. One way to obtain information on interests and learning styles is to administer learning inventories.

Teachers can create their own inventories or consult samples that are readily available on the Internet. By searching for "learning style inventories," teachers can obtain free inventories that they can administer and interpret. One such site is www.learning-style-online.com/inventory/. Multiple inventories for both personal interests and learning styles can be found at the Survey Monkey website, www.SurveyMonkey.com. Teachers report that this site is easy to use and allows them to create their own surveys or inventories using the online tools provided. The site also includes tools to help teachers analyze the survey data collected. There is, however, a fee for using this site. Other commercial sites that provide a similar service are www.instantsurvey.com and www.zoomerang.com. Specific learning style inventories that assess multiple intelligences can be found online by conducting a general search for "multiple intelligences surveys." Teachers can also conduct an online search for "interest inventories."

Examples of teacher-created assessment inventories can be found in *Differentiated Instruction in the English Classroom: Content, Process, Product, and Assessment* (King-Shaver and Hunter 2003). In addition to administering interest and learning style inventories, teachers can obtain information about student interests by simply asking the students directly. This can be done as a prompted journal entry or sponge activity at the beginning of class. The following is a list of writing prompts on student interests:

- In your spare time, what types of music do you like to listen to?
- If you could travel anywhere, where would it be?
- If you were required to read any book, what type would you prefer?

- What school activities, sports, or clubs do you participate in?

- What types of movies or TV shows do you like to watch?

- What should I know about you to help you learn better?

Performance Assessments

Performance assessments provide students with the opportunity to demonstrate their learning through a variety of products in different modes. For this reason, performance assessments can support differentiation based on both readiness and learning styles. Insofar as possible, performance assessments try to duplicate activities that people engage in outside of school. Rubrics or scoring guides accompany performance assessments so students can have a clear understanding of how their products will be assessed. Performance assessments may be small activities within or at the end of a classroom unit, or they can be major course requirements across the school.

The following performance assessment is based on a framework Grant Wiggins and Jay McTighe developed to help teachers create performance assessments called GRASPS: goal, role, audience, situation, product, standards (2005, 159).

The English Department in your school is considering adding more multicultural literature to the curriculum. The problem is that if more texts are added, some texts will have to be cut from the required curriculum. A parent has proposed that Shakespeare's *Romeo and Juliet* be taken off the required reading list because it is dated and written in a language no longer used. Students who have read and studied the play in their English classes have been asked to write letters to the English department, expressing their views on this subject. The English department values student opinions and will take the student letters into consideration when deciding whether *Romeo and Juliet* should continue to be a required text for 9th grade English.

The Wiggins and McTighe model can be used to differentiate assessment products. In the above example, the product can be changed from a letter written to the English Department to an oral presentation at a department meeting. A student might also develop a PowerPoint presentation on the topic.

It is the responsibility and obligation of educators to determine and design assessments that truly support and celebrate each learner. Differentiated assessment is the logical and mandatory result of differentiated instruction. Differentiated assessment, like differentiated instruction, should address content, process, and product as well as students' needs, abilities, experiences, and learning styles.

Reading and Differentiated Instruction

The concept of teaching reading to adolescents, historically, has been relegated either to remedial classes for those who cannot yet decode words or synthesize meaning from words and sentences or to accelerated classes for those who want to increase their reading speed in order to be ready to read more quickly when they go to college. Although it is still true that middle and secondary educators need to address reading as an act of learning in itself, this has been replaced by concentration on the concept of reading to learn. In other words, middle and high school students need to be taught and encouraged to attack reading as a thinking skill that challenges them before, during, and after reading to make connections with text, between texts, with their own lives, and with the world around them. In addition, with the increased pressure from state assessments and future employers, educators like Willard Daggett (2005) warn teachers and students that in order to succeed in the world of 2015 and beyond, they must be able to read increasingly complex texts. It does not matter whether the format is a traditional paper book or an interactive e-book. Comprehension and understanding of what another has written are essential.

Carolyn Chapman and Rita King (2003) provide guidance that is useful for English language arts teachers on aspects of both learning to read and reading to learn. With regard to learning to read, Chapman and King stress the need for teachers to begin with shorter passages, to model comprehension strategies, and to use personal student stories and writing to engage the struggling readers. Using a standardized test of reading or doing a running record by recording students' reading habits as they read aloud to the teacher are ways to determine whether students are struggling, successful, or fluent readers. Once the teacher makes this determination, the diagnosis requires action, and differentiated instruction is the action that leads each student to improve. Selection of teaching and learning materials is crucial at this juncture. Teachers have used various texts with differing reading levels to address the same unit and lesson objectives. Additionally, an assessment strategy that works well with struggling readers is choice boards, in which readers select work to be completed. Some teachers even create a variety of choice boards that all look alike to a casual observer but are constructed with different levels of activities and questions to support different learners' needs, readiness, and learning styles. Such teachers truly practice the belief that differentiated instruction leads to and is judged by differentiated assessment. Such assessment allows students to celebrate what they do know instead of being disparaged for what they do not understand.

However, learning to read is not usually the primary communal objective for reading instruction at the middle and high school levels; instead, teaching students to read to learn is the objective, with responsibility shared across all content areas. However, many secondary educators see this objective as relegated to the English language arts teachers. They say, "After all, isn't reading all kids do in English language arts class? It's not my job. I have so much science, math, social studies content to cover!" Such naysayers fail to understand that reading is essential to content comprehension in all subjects. Cris Tovani (2004a) addresses issues and presents practices for reading strategy infusion in grades 6–12 in her aptly titled book *Do I Really Have to Teach Reading?* Moreover, English language arts teachers should not chastise themselves because they do not know reading strategies. Most have had little or no training or courses in prereading, during-reading, and postreading strategies. The Council of Chief State School Officers (2007) in their most practical "Adolescent Literacy Toolkit" acknowledges that English language arts is a subject distinct from reading. This toolkit and its accompanying website present a summary of literacy instructional practices that range from analytic graphic organizers to interactive word walls to think-alouds with high school learners. This website also presents three lesson plans and narratives that demonstrate the teaching of reading in the content area of English language arts. Each of these lessons provides students with thinking activities and strategies that will help them become proficient and fluent readers, particularly if teachers adapt them to differentiate instruction. Tovani (2004b) and other reading researchers have identified that good readers utilize certain thinking habits and patterns when they read: they activate prior knowledge, question the text and themselves, draw inferences, distinguish between important and unimportant information, and know how to "fix up" the text so understanding increases. Teachers can differentiate instruction to help learners acquire or enhance each of these habits and patterns. Differentiation can be considered and employed before reading, during the process, and after reading.

Differentiated Instruction and Before-Reading Strategies

Prereading strategies help students set a purpose for their reading, motivate them to read, and also lead to more and stronger comprehension of what they do read. Employing prereading strategies helps teachers access students' prior knowledge of a topic or content. When teachers understand this background information, they use it to differentiate content, process, or product for each learner.

The role of prior knowledge was largely ignored in middle and high school education until the 1970s when educators, through their research, began to realize the role that "schema" plays in reading comprehension (Smith 1978). *Schemata*, the plural form of *schema*, are the categories individuals develop in their brains as information is stored—mental filing cabinets, if you will. When students read, different schemata are activated, which means that file drawers are opened and new knowledge is connected to prior knowledge. In other words, this knowledge is stored in files that the individual student's brain decides are connected. The result is comprehension.

Understanding that there are two distinct yet interrelated major types of prior knowledge is essential for teachers who choose to differentiate instruction. Students can have prior knowledge of the content or background knowledge of the text structure. Teachers can help students learn to activate both types of knowledge by providing them direct instruction, either individually or collectively as needed. Two popular before-reading activities that help to activate learners' prior knowledge of content and help teachers to differentiate starting points for instruction are anticipation guides and KWL (What I *Know*, What I *Want* to Know, What I *Learned*) charts. Anticipation guides motivate learners as they create interest in a subject to be studied and assist students as they recall what they already know (Smith 1978). These guides consist of lists of statements about the content and concepts that will be in the reading. Students indicate whether they agree, disagree, or are unsure about each statement. Teachers can use the answers on the anticipation guides to differentiate, to determine what needs to be taught or compacted so it is not explicitly taught to individual students, groups, or the entire class. After reading, students can return to the same anticipation guide and decide whether their answers remain the same or can change their responses to indicate what they now know. Teachers can use this comparison of pre- and postreading beliefs to spark animated class discussions not only about the content but also about the reading process that caused students to affirm or contradict their first answers. Additionally, based on what is learned, teachers can tailor the next assignments to fit different levels of readiness or interests. For example, based on students' responses to the anticipation guide for *Julius Caesar* (Figure 4–1) and the discussion of answers to this guide after reading, teachers can divide the class into groups to research unresolved issues. Some students could pursue an intertextual study by reading a text related to the issues or historical facts raised by their reading of the play. Other students or groups of learners could read another play by Shakespeare and compare it to *Julius Caesar* or watch various film versions of the play and write comparisons of the films to the play. Others could read and contrast a historical account of the events with the drama. To create anticipation guides, teachers need to preview materials to be read and identify major content and concepts and make a list of five to ten general statements related to this content and these concepts. The actual guides need to have places and a code for students to indicate whether they agree, disagree, or are unsure. Learners read and mark guides before they read the assignment. Students read the text and return to guides to verify their original answers.

In addition to the use of anticipation guides as a way to activate learners' prior knowledge and to differentiate instruction, teachers can utilize one of the popular

Figure 4–1

Anticipation Guide for Shakespeare's *Julius Caesar*

Directions to students: Place an "A" on the line next to each statement if you agree with it and a "D" if you disagree. We will return to this guide after you have read the play.

Before Reading	Statement	After Reading
_____	People can be convinced to act against their beliefs.	_____
_____	The ends justify the means.	_____
_____	There are times when it is right to break the law.	_____
_____	Flattery is a dangerous thing.	_____
_____	People are responsible for their own lives. Fate has nothing to do with it.	_____

variations of the KWL charts (Ogle 1986). These charts present students with a topic, theme, or concept that is included in the assigned reading. In a classic KWL, each of the three categories is written at the top of a sheet of paper and readers fill in the information independently under each of the first two categories before they read. This writing on the chart helps readers to remember what they already know and to facilitate the opening of their brains' file cabinets—schemata. Some teachers refine the What I Know column by dividing it into two categories—What I Know I Know and What I Think I Know. This distinction asks learners to employ critical thinking skills as they distinguish what they are sure of from what they believe. After reading, some teachers add a column: What I Still Want to Learn. Using this information, teachers can help students continue their learning about the topic by using this column's answers to direct and differentiate research projects. For example, when introducing a unit on literature written by Indian and Indian American authors, students are asked to list what they know about the customs of India in the column or columns acknowledging what they know or think they know. Next, they list what they would like to learn about the topic. Teachers can differentiate instruction at this point by selecting readings based on student readiness and interests as students report on their KWL columns. Some students can be assigned nonfiction accounts of Indian culture and customs. Others can be given newspaper articles or other narratives written by Indian or Indian American authors. In any case, readers return to their charts and record what they have learned about Indian customs and culture. Students can compare their lists after the first column or columns have been completed and again after they have completed the third column. During class discussions as students share their lists, the differences in knowledge and learning are revealed. Teachers can use this information to differentiate assignments, for example, by assigning different texts to read. Specifically with regard to Indian and Indian American writers, the works of Anita Desai, R. K. Narayan, Bharati Mukerjee, Indu Sundaresan, Jhumpa Lahiri, Amitav Ghosh, Chitra Banerjee Divakaruni, and Vikram Seth should be considered, depending on the maturity level of the readers. KWL is an effective prereading strategy because it engages learners by activating prior knowledge and raises their interest in the topic or work of literature to be studied. This is accomplished not only by creating individual prereading lists but also by class discussions based on these lists.

Teachers can help learners comprehend and understand reading by activating their background knowledge through such activities as anticipation guides and KWL charts, but they can also help learners comprehend and understand reading by assisting them in analyzing text structure. Jim Burke (2000) provides directions for analyzing types of text structure, such as poetry, essays, newspaper articles, speeches, websites, letters, novels, biographies, and nonfiction. He instructs teachers to work with learners to identify the purpose of texts as informational, persuasive, explanatory, and multipurpose. Additionally, Burke lists elements of the text such as the author, credibility, elements, devices, components, conventions, and structure that need to be considered. Concerning differentiation, students may need varying amounts of direct instruction and scaffolded support of text structure analyses based on preassessment of readiness levels.

Differentiated Instruction and During-Reading Strategies

English teachers can employ differentiated strategies to individualize the process as students read and interact with text. Guiding students to identify different types of questions is a metacognitive strategy that can increase understanding and comprehension during reading. QAR (Question-Answer Relationship) is a strategy that asks readers to analyze the relationship between questions and answers according to whether the answers are right in the text ("right there"), require readers to make inferences and fit ideas from the text together ("think and search"), ask readers to utilize outside knowledge and apply it to what is read ("author and you"), or require readers to relate information and ideas in the text to their own experiences ("on my own") (Raphael and Pearson 1982). Students not only answer questions but also analyze the type of questions. This strategy can be tailored to individual student needs. Those whom the teacher diagnoses as having adequate prior knowledge and reading ability can be asked to explain the higher-order, inference questions and answers. Those who can succeed at the literal level could be asked to provide the answers and relationship between questions and answers at the comprehension level. The following list correlates the four types of questions and their relationship to Benjamin Bloom's Taxonomy (1956).

right there (knowledge): "What is . . .", "How many . . .", "Who is . . .", "List . . ."
think and search (comprehension and application): "The main idea is . . .",
    "Compare . . .", "Contrast . . ."
author and you (analysis): "The speaker's attitude is . . .", "This passage
    implies . . .", "The reason why . . ."
on my own (evaluation and synthesis): "In your opinion . . .", "Based on what you
    know . . .", "How might . . .", "What if . . ."

Coding text in a variety of ways and models can also help readers to interact and react to text. Stephanie Harvey and Anne Goudvis (2007) suggest the following list to be used for coding text: R = reminds me of, T-T = text-to-text connection, L = new learning, $?$ = question, $*$ = key idea, $!$ = surprising information, and I = inference. Harvey and Goudvis also suggest that for some students, doing the text coding can be disruptive as it interferes with the fluency of their reading. For these students, they suggest recording on sticky notes. Also, students can be encouraged to reread a paragraph or short section and then code it. Some teachers use a specific coding strategy to help learners read persuasive writing. Text codes include: i = information, d = description, p = persuasion, v = author's voice or word choice indicates point of view, and $?$ = question or don't understand

(57). Teachers can use the coding strategies to differentiate instruction. Each student or group of students can be assigned a different code. They all report out on a coding data summary sheet to tally results and give a graphic descriptor of the reading and its viewpoint.

Natalie Miller, an English teacher at West Morris Central High School (New Jersey), takes quite seriously her role as a teacher who helps students read to learn so that they can develop proficient and fluent understanding of text. Miller designed and implements a during-reading lesson to include differentiation and reading to learn. It focuses on distinguishing "need to know" from "nice to know" information, a task that ninth graders in particular find difficult. She reads aloud with students during Acts I and II of *Romeo and Juliet.* Anxious to determine their ability to grasp Shakespearean language on their own, she created a guided note sheet to distinguish "need to know" (listed in the left column) and "nice to know" (listed in the right column). The teacher further guides student note taking and use of the chart by breaking the categories into smaller chunks for those who need it, such as dramatic irony, illusion, and pun for literary devices. The teacher believes that this process helps learners focus their attention on the most important aspects of the text and, more importantly, gives them more confidence as solo readers.

Laura Pelizzoni, an English teacher at West Morris Mendham High School (New Jersey), uses the RAFT strategy (role, audience, format, topic) during reading to differentiate instruction (Santa 1988). Students use this strategy frequently to improve achievement both during and after reading and writing. They identify the writer's role, audience, format required, and topic for their essays, particularly the persuasive essays that are required on the state assessment test. With regard to reading, the students transfer their knowledge of RAFT from their own writing to examine an author's purpose and effectiveness. The teacher uses this strategy effectively with Mark Twain's *Huckleberry Finn* as she challenges adolescents of varying reading abilities and interests to look at Twain's purpose for writing the novel.

Learning stations, the differentiating strategy that asks learners to work on a series of assignments for a specific period of time, are also successful to get adolescents to interact with text during reading. Figure 4–2 demonstrates a learning station activity to help middle school students relate to the novel *Hoot* by Carl Hiaasen and to expand their understanding through the reading of nonfiction.

Figure 4–2

Stations for *Hoot* by Carl Hiaasen

Directions to students: You will be working in stations today. Everyone is required to complete station two. You need to complete three additional stations, for a total of four stations. You do not have to complete the stations in any particular order. The directions and the materials you need are at each station. Please check the clock and pace yourself. When you finish, put all your material into your folder to be collected and assessed. If you finish before the end of the period, work on an anchor activity.

Teacher's note: You can differentiate by assigning certain stations to students.

Station One
You are Roy, and after your adventures with the running boy and the burrowing owls, you write a letter to your best friend in Montana. Explain to your friend how you now feel about living in Florida and tell him why you feel this way.

Station Two
At this station, you will read an article about an endangered species. Take a worksheet from this station and answer the questions about the article.

Station Three
The empty lot that serves as home for the owls' nests is described in the novel. Draw an illustration for this section of the book.

Station Four
Choose five vocabulary words from the box and write a sentence about the novel for each word. Your sentences must show you know the meaning of the words.

Station Five
You are a student in Roy's class. Write five questions you want to ask Roy and explain how the answers will help you understand better what happened.

Station Six
What are some other possible solutions to the dilemma of the burrowing owls? Identify two and explain why each would work.

Station Seven
Complete a graphic organizer for a character in the story other than Roy.

Station Eight
Using the worksheet provided, make text-to-self, text-to-world, and text-to-text connections to the novel.

Students are required to read a nonfiction article, but they are allowed choice—a hallmark of differentiated instruction that most appeals to adolescents—as to which three of the other seven stations they will complete.

Jennifer Stanislawczyk, a teacher at Crossroads South Middle School in South Brunswick, New Jersey, uses a variation of the learning station strategy as she plans and implements a twenty-six-word vocabulary lesson using the planning guide suggested in this book. Figure 4–3 contains this guide, and Figure 4–4 presents the tasks she created to challenge and celebrate different learning styles.

Literature circles, as proposed and proliferated by Harvey Daniels (2002), have become very popular with teachers who believe in differentiation. These circles are small, temporary, flexible groups that can be tailored to take advantage of students' interests and learning styles while also addressing their readiness and background knowledge deficits. Students assume or are assigned roles, such as questioner, summarizer, connector, literary luminary, illustrator, researcher, and word wizard. In their circles, learners, during or after reading, discuss the content and implications of what they are reading or have read. As teachers differentiate instruction, they can determine a range of texts that can be used for different groups during the same unit of study. Text sets are a popular way to differentiate instruction when using literature circles. Groups studying text sets can be formed based on an author, genre, theme, or readiness levels. Natalie Miller of West Morris Central High School diagnoses and considers carefully and reflectively how to help make complex reading understandable and frequently uses critiques to help learners understand an author's intent and motivation. She modifies and adapts the differentiated instruction strategy of literature circles to help tenth-grade students understand a difficult article written by Arthur Miller, entitled "Are You Now or Were You Ever?" The teacher feels the article explains some of Arthur Miller's thinking behind composing the play, *The Crucible*, and it is an important primary source about a writer's motivation. Yet the teacher worries that students might be confused by the vocabulary and by the article's two main ideas. Natalie deliberately places her students into groups to differentiate instruction, and each student has to perform three of four roles during the reading sharing and process. The article is read in three parts, and for each part a student has a different role, as in literature circles, of summarizer, questioner, clarifier, or predictor. After each student shares his or her role, the group discusses the section's contents. Then they move on to the next

Figure 4–3

Planning Guide and Tasks for Vocabulary and Multiple Intelligences

Course Title and Level: Grade 7–8 English
Unit: Word Study

Essential Questions

How can new, higher-level vocabulary words become more deeply ingrained in everyday use?

Unit-Specific Questions

How can multiple intelligences support vocabulary learning?

Knowledge/Skills

Students will know:
    How to use vocabulary words in content

Students will be able to:
    Gain a deeper understanding of the word study vocabulary
    Demonstrate correct context usage through creative means

Modes of Differentiation Used

Process
    Flexible grouping, flexible time

Products
    Choice of tasks

Based on (readiness, interests, learning styles)

    Interests
    Learning styles

Strategies: stations—student choice, cooperative learning groups, oral presentations

Developed by Jennifer Stanislawczyk, Crossroads Middle School South, South Brunswick, New Jersey

Figure 4–4

Word Study and Multiple Intelligences

Directions for students: Complete a vocabulary project by choosing one of the tasks.

Note to teachers: A variation is to require students to complete two projects from two different categories.

Word Smart

Use all twenty-six vocabulary words in context. Submit a final copy with the vocabulary underlined. Choices: a vignette, a news article, journal entries, letters from one character in a book to another.

Logic Smart

Compose a series of poems, using one or more of the following forms: haiku, sonnet, diamante.

Art Smart

Create a visual by choosing one of the following options. Utilize all twenty-six words. Label your illustration by using the vocabulary words. Choices: a poster with drawings, pictures, or photos; a 3-D model using clay or other material.

Music Smart

Choose a popular song and change the lyrics or write an original song or rap. Utilize all twenty-six words in context. Submit a typed final copy of your song with the vocabulary underlined. Perform your song live in class or make a music video.

People Smart

Create a game or group participation activity utilizing all twenty-six words. Involve all class members in the game or activity. Submit typed directions for the game or activity and hand in all game materials.

Nature Smart

Bring twenty-six items from nature to display in class. Write a description for each. All twenty-six words must be used when the descriptions are competed. Type labels for your display with the vocabulary words underlined.

Technology Smart

Create a PowerPoint slideshow that includes all twenty-six words, their definitions, and sentences with the words used in context. Your PowerPoint should also include visuals, such as clip art.

section, exchange roles, and finally complete the summarizing questions, "What message is the author sending? What does he want readers to know?" The teacher consciously plans this lesson not only to be differentiated but also to incorporate the reading to learn skills of questioning the text and drawing inferences.

When students are reading independently or preparing material for their cooperative groups such as literature circles, teachers can meet with students who need more direct instruction in literacy skills and strategies and present minilessons or brief reviews of the identified needs. For example, some students may need specific vocabulary instruction so that when they return to their literature circles they can participate successfully.

Differentiated Instruction and After-Reading Strategies

Teachers can choose to create after-reading activities that are differentiated for students, to have them question, summarize, and assess what they have read. As her class concludes reading a novel, Cara Kober, an English teacher at West Morris Mendham High School (New Jersey), meets the needs of each learner by using a variation of "word sort," a vocabulary activity that asks students to determine categories for words as they sort them into "like" configurations. The activity can be used before, during, or after reading to make adolescents critically think about how words are related in a given unit of study. Cara adapts the word sort activity to make it a summary strategy to discuss key concepts of Ralph Ellison's *Invisible Man*. The teacher writes five key concepts in red on five separate index cards and prepares a set for each of the four groups. Key concepts for this novel include the motif of blindness, the genre of bildungsroman, existentialism, identity, and episodic. The teacher then writes subconcepts in black ink on one card for each term: Jack's glass eye, choice, Reverend Barbee, Dr. Bledsoe, yams, absurdity, surrealism, dreams, manhole, speeches, Brotherhood, Mary Rambo, Clifton, genre, pattern, selfhood, development, Optic White, ECT, accepting the past, grandfather's advice, and so on. The cards are placed into a bag labeled "invisible man." Students are put into groups according to the teacher's informal diagnosis of their ability to demonstrate what they have learned. Identical bags are distributed to each group. Groups are given fifteen minutes to organize and "lay out" the cards before time is frozen. Then each group presents their organization and others ask them questions about why they categorized as they did. Cara found that some students experience stress over "what answer is right," even though they are instructed that there is not necessarily one correct answer. The teacher also reports that comments like "I never thought of that angle" and "Now that they explained it, that makes sense" are heard during the spirited discussions that this word sort activity generates.

Another useful postreading strategy is a learning station activity that can be differentiated to have students react to summer reading. Figure 4–5 details seven stations that challenge students to choose what they want to do to tell about what they learned. They can select a graphic organizer, draw a book cover, or write to a variety of different prompts. Using this book report learning station activity to assess summer reading not only provides a way to differentiate student responses but also can give teachers additional knowledge about each learner at the start of the school year. If a student selects station seven, which asks him or her to make connections to prior reading, teachers can learn about this learner's background knowledge and readiness for readings during the current school year.

Deliberately placing students into groups such as the word sort activity, designing learning stations such as the summer reading stations, and using peer groups such as literature circles are hallmarks of differentiated instruction. Another activity involving deliberately placing students into groups based on their interests and readiness is the Socratic Seminar (Adler 1982). This activity has likewise become a hallmark of differentiated instruction because teachers can assign students varying levels of questions, from comprehension to evaluation, based on students' readiness and understanding of the concepts or book to be discussed. Socratic Seminar is a discussion strategy that emphasizes student questioning and responding to each other. Rebecca Kipp-Newbold, West Morris Central High School (New Jersey) teacher, frequently uses this strategy. She begins with the following directive to her students: " 'Wisdom begins in wonder.'—Socrates. A Socratic Seminar uses the pedagogical philosophy of Socrates: true learning comes through the process of questioning. In this discussion, you work to maintain a balance between asking open-ended questions and posing possible answers. Students should fill out the Preparation for the Socratic Seminar Sheet to get ready for the discussion. Students who are absent on the day of their assigned discussion must still turn in their notes for the missed discussion. They must also participate in the Make-Up Discussion (TBA)." This Preparation for the Socratic Seminar Sheet (Figure 4–6) is accompanied

Figure 4–5

Stations for Independent and Summer Reading

(90-minute block)

Directions to students: You will be working in stations today. Everyone is required to complete station one. You need to complete three additional stations, for a total of four of the eight presented. You do not have to complete the stations in any particular order. The directions and the materials you need are at each station.

Remember to take your folder with you and put all your completed work into the folder to be collected. You should also take a copy of the book you read with you to each station. Watch the time so that you can pace yourself and complete the four stations today. If you finish before the block is over, you may work on revising/editing a paper in your writing folder.

Station One: Theme

Select a quotation card from the box. In a few paragraphs, explain how this quotation could apply to the book your read.

Station Two: Illustration

You have been asked to illustrate the book cover for a new edition of the book you read. The cover should illustrate a significant scene, image, character, or symbol from the book. On the back of the cover, briefly explain the significance of your illustration.

Station Three: Open-Ended Questions

If you had the opportunity to speak with the author, what two meaningful questions would you ask him or her about the book? Explain how his or her answer to your questions would help you understand the book better.

continued on next page

Figure 4–5   *continued from previous page*

Station Four: Characters

Select one of the graphic organizers at this station and complete it for a major character in the book your read. On the back of the graphic organizer, write a brief character analysis of the person you selected.

Station Five: Figurative Language

Find an excerpt from your book that contains powerful figurative language. Copy the sentences in which literary devices are used and identify what type(s) they are. Select one sentence you copied and write a paragraph explaining how it enhances the theme, plot, characters, or any combination of the three.

Station Six: Vocabulary

Choose five words from the word bank and write a paragraph in which you apply these words to your book. You should consider the theme(s), plot, and characters. Your writing must show that you know the meaning of the words.

Station Seven: Connections

Use the chart to identify three connections you can make between this book and other texts you have read. On the back of the sheet, explain one of these connections in detail. In what ways is this book similar to another text? What do the similarities show?

Station Eight: Quotations

Select three key quotations from the book your read. Briefly explain why each of the quotations you selected is significant. Consider: What does the quotation reveal about character? How does it contribute to the plot? How does it help to develop the theme?

Variation

Teachers may give students *individual task cards* that assign the students to some specific stations. These required stations can differ for students based on the students' readiness, interests, or learning styles. There should still be some element of choice built into the stations.

Figure 4–6

Preparation for the Socratic Seminar

Student's name: _____ Topic: _____

1. Complete the sentence: This is really a text about . . .

2. Pick a passage that confuses or interests you and create questions that relate to this passage. Include phrases such as "Why do you think . . ." and "What do you believe is the significance of . . ." Then, propose possible answers.

  Passage:_____

Open-Ended Questions	Possible Answers

3. Select an important symbol from your section of the reading and create questions that surround this symbol. Then, propose possible answers.

  Symbol: _____

Open-Ended Questions	Possible Answers

4. Select anything else of interest/confusion from the text; create questions and propose possible answers.

  Topic:_____

Open-Ended Questions	Possible Answers

by a five-point rubric that judges students' performance on questioning, use of evidence, and speaking and listening. Rebecca frequently uses the "inner-outer circle" technique to help her manage the discussion in a class of twenty-five or more pupils (Ball and Brewer 2000).

Students on the inside of the circle prepare to participate in the seminar by filling out the Preparation for the Socratic Seminar Sheet and by marking their books with removable sticky notes. The seminar begins with students sharing their responses to the first question: This is really a text about . . . From there, students are free to direct the conversation to areas of interest or confusion using the questions they prepared (Preparation for the Socratic Seminar Sheet). Generally, seminars last twenty to thirty minutes. Those on the outside of the circle either take notes on the seminar or write in their journals about questions raised in the seminar. The teacher checks these notes and gives students credit for this activity as well. Outer circle members give feedback to participants in the inner circle, but Rebecca has found that both the students and she prefer the note taking. Also, an empty seat is usually left in the seminar circle, which permits one student from the outside to join the seminar. The student is allowed to ask one question or make one comment after being acknowledged by someone in the seminar. This empty seat has become very popular. Rebecca reports, "Socratic Seminars work really well for me: they empower quieter students to participate in a structured way; they ask students to work cooperatively to create meaning; they ask students to balance actively listening with active discussion."

Some students, particularly visual learners, benefit from completing graphic organizers after reading a text. Graphic organizers help readers understand text structure and identify literary elements. Graphic organizers such as cause and effect charts are especially helpful for understanding the text structure in content area textbooks and nonfiction articles. Popular graphic organizers such as Venn diagrams for comparing two characters, character trait charts, and plot outlines help students clarify their thinking as they construct a visual representation of their understanding. Many websites contain examples of graphic organizers for all grade levels. Teachers who want a starting place can also consult *Graphic Organizers and Activities for Differentiated Instruction in Reading* (Witherell and McMackin 2002). The choice board in Figure 4–7 offers graphic organizers as one of multiple ways readers can demonstrate their understanding of text.

Adolescent Literacy and Differentiated Instruction

Figure 4–7

Choice Board for Narrative Text

Directions for students: You are to complete one task from each column. All tasks should be written.

Note to teachers: This can be a free choice board or you can assign rows and use it as a tiered activity.

Character	Conflict	Theme
Complete a character chart for the main character and another one for the antagonist in the story.	Write a paragraph explaining the main conflict in the story and how it is resolved.	Explain the main idea or theme of the story in a paragraph.
Complete a Venn diagram comparing the protagonist in this story to one in another book, play, or short story.	Select three key events in the story that show the main conflict and explain briefly what each reveals.	Select a passage in the book that supports the main idea or theme and explain how it does this.
Find three scenes that help define the character through his or her actions or words and explain how they do this.	Explain how the choices the protagonist makes affect the conflict and its resolution.	Compare the main idea or theme in this story to the theme in another story, play, or book.

The lessons described here help adolescents become independent, strategic readers and learners. The strategies presented in this chapter help students learn to read and read to learn. New technologies that impact adolescent readers are presented in Chapter 8. The following section introduces a multimodal text structure that presents new opportunities and new challenges for the adolescent reader.

Differentiated Instruction and Graphic Novels

On any given weekend afternoon in many book stores across the country, adolescents can be seen sitting on the floor between stacks of books reading. Some may be reading alone, and others are sharing the texts in front of them. Many can be seen smiling and even laughing aloud. They seem totally focused and oblivious to their surroundings. What has captured their attention with such intensity? These young people are reading and sharing books from the shelves labeled "graphic novels" and "manga." These adolescents are totally engaged in reading genres that were unknown to most readers and teachers ten years ago. As Donna Alvermann

(2007) notes, "Adolescents find their own reasons for becoming literate . . . their definition of reading is perhaps broader than the schools" (19). Graphic novels, which appeal to many adolescents, are a popular genre that is gaining acceptance in school curricula.

Many teachers were introduced to graphic novels with the publication of the Pulitzer Prize–winning story of a Holocaust survivor, *Maus: A Survivor's Tale* by Art Spiegelman (1986), later to become *Maus I: A Survivor's Tale,* followed by *Maus II* in 1991. The two volumes tell of the survival of the author's father during the Holocaust. Both texts show how graphic novels can address a serious topic with literary and educational value. English and social studies teachers today use these two books to introduce issues surrounding the Holocaust through words and images. The publication of *Maus* in 1986 changed the way many educators viewed graphic novels, moving them from superhero comics to serious literature.

A study of the roots of graphic novels traces their form back to medieval times in Europe and the *Bayeux Tapestry,* which graphically depicts the Norman invasion of Britain in a sequential format. In Asia, the form is traced to scrolls created in the same time period that depict the life of Buddha (Fingeroth 2008, 11). Sequential graphic story telling continued in various forms until it reached its heyday in the 1940s and 1950s in the form of comic books. In 1941, comic books ventured into literature with the publication of Classics Illustrated, a series of comics that presented condensed versions of classic books such as *Don Quixote* (Fingeroth 2008, 14). Most educators did not take Classics Illustrated seriously; graphic novels changed their view.

Graphic novels and mangas, the Japanese form, may have evolved from comic books, but they are more sophisticated. Although their content is similar, mangas are read from the back to the front, from right to left, challenging some first-time readers. In this chapter, the term *graphic novels* is an umbrella term applying to both graphic novels and mangas. Graphic novels are generally longer than comic books and are bound in book form. Gene Yang (2008) humorously defines graphic novels as "thick comic books," echoing Art Spiegelman's definition, " a comic book that you need a bookmark for" (Fingeroth 2008, 5). Graphic novels go beyond most comic books by presenting intricate narrative plot structures and fully developed characters. But graphic novels are not limited to narratives; they are also biographies, autobiographies, and informational texts. Yang (2008) displayed the versatility of the graphic novel form by presenting his entire article for the *Language Arts* journal in an illustrated serial panel format. All forms of graphic novels include illustrations, usually black and white, that complement the written word. Graphic novels can be used in the classroom to support literacy learning. Teri Lesesne (2007) found that graphic novels provide "visual scaffolds that help reluctant or struggling readers get hooked and continue" to read (67). She supports using graphic novels to supplement classroom texts because they not only provide motivation, but also support multiple ways of knowing. Visual learners, in particular, are drawn to texts with multiple illustrations to support the narrative. In their study of adolescent male readers, Michael Smith and Jeff Wilhelm (2002) found that the visual appeal of graphic novels makes them one of the few genres that consistently engage male readers. Graphic novels appeal to a wide range of young readers because adolescents find them more accessible than most classic works of literature. This is not surprising as they are closer to other popular media such as television. As Yang notes, "By combining image and text, graphic novels bridge the gap between media we watch and media we read" (2008, 187).

Graphic novels are a good complement to traditional print texts in the classroom. James Carter (2007) offers a reason for this in the introduction to his book *Building Literacy Connections with Graphic Novels*: "Reading a graphic novel is closer to reading a traditional prose book or magazine than reading other visual media such as weblogs or instant messaging" (xii). The range of graphic novels available today is so great that, as Carter claims, "There is a graphic novel for virtually every learner in your English language arts classroom" (1). This is very appealing to teachers who want to differentiate instruction. Graphic novels provide an opportunity for teachers to differentiate both content and product. The content in a literature study can be differentiated by providing graphic novels as choices for a class or small-group study of literature. Graphic novels can be read independently or as companion texts to more traditional selections. When differentiating product, teachers can offer students the choice to produce their own texts in graphic novel form.

Teachers have expressed a concern that graphic novels may contain too much violence, sexually specific material, or offensive language. Some graphic novels do. Teachers need to be familiar with the texts their students are choosing to read. Carter provides a good starting point for identifying graphic novels that are appropriate for classroom use. The school librarian or media specialist is another good resource for bibliographies of graphic novels. In fact, many school librarians were the first to champion graphic novels for inclusion in the schools. Some websites also provide information on graphic novels for teachers and parents. Two helpful sites are: http://publishersweekly.com and www.libraryjournal.com.

Teachers should not let concerns about content stop them from introducing graphic novels into their curricula. Offering our students reading selections they can connect with helps to make them lifelong readers.

One way teachers are using graphic novels is by pairing them with traditional texts and creating intertextual studies that can aid comprehension; "intertextuality plays an important role in the construction of meaning and the intertextual links students make enrich their understanding of both texts" (King-Shaver 2005, 9). Multiple examples of graphic novels and traditional text pairings are included in Carter's book (2007), such as Hawthorne's *The Scarlet Letter* and Katherine Arnoldi's *The Amazing "True" Story of a Teenage Single Mom*; Dante's *Inferno* and an X-Men story; and a graphic novel visualization of *Beowulf* by Gareth Hinds. J. D. Schraffenberger explains how the graphic novel adaptation of *Beowulf* makes the epic more appealing and understandable for today's adolescent reader, concluding that this graphic version not only lightens "some of the 'load' of the text, but the comic also helps fill in gaps of knowledge for students about the aristocratic warrior culture of the poem" (Carter 2007, 69). This example of *Beowulf* shows how graphic novels can promote literacy by introducing students to advanced literature, texts they might not otherwise read or be able to fully comprehend. Because a large number of classic works of literature have been recreated as graphic novels, teachers can use them when differentiating literature studies. There are times when the teacher may want to use a graphic novel and a paired classic text for a whole-class study, but there are also times when giving students choice in selecting the pairs can be motivational. When students are motivated to read, they are more likely to pay close attention to the text and their comprehension improves.

Another way graphic novels are used to promote literacy is to introduce or review literary devices and narrative structure. An article entitled "Using Comics and Graphic Novels in the Classroom" (2005) noted the effectiveness of using graphic novels for teaching literary features, asserting that graphic novels can be used effectively for teaching narrative structure, because, like novels, "They have a beginning, middle and end as well as a main character that develops through conflicts and the story's climax." Douglas Fisher and Nancy Frey (2007) have also found that teachers can use graphic novels to introduce literary concepts and devices by providing a less challenging text for analysis as students are learning. For example, they cite using *Persepolis* by Marjane Satrapi (2003) when studying elements of autobiography. *Maus I* and *Maus II* (Spiegelman 1986, 1991), mentioned earlier, are among graphic novels that can be used to study author's voice in autobiography. *Bone* by Jeff Smith (2004) is an award-winning nine-volume graphic novel that was rated by *Time* magazine as one of the top ten graphic novels of all time (Fingeroth 2008, 85). *Bone* is so well crafted, both visually and verbally, that many of the literary devices taught in middle school and high school English language arts classes can be taught when studying it, including literary allusions, symbolism, imagery, and character development. *Bone* can also be paired with classic epics such as *The Odyssey* for a study of the hero's quest. Reading graphic novels with a critical eye can help students develop the skills they need to read more challenging texts.

Teachers can differentiate instruction when teaching literary analysis using graphic novels by first preassessing their students' understanding of literary elements. Then, through curriculum compacting or tiered tasks, students can work on the literary elements they need to reinforce or move on to application. For example, basic readers may be asked to find visual clues that contribute to character development in a section of a graphic novel, while advanced readers may be asked to trace a motif in both words and images throughout the graphic novel. Basic readers may work with the teacher to identify the narrative structure in the graphic novel, while advanced readers compare visual and verbal clues to identify mood in a significant scene. Figures 4–8 and 4–9 present a planning guide and a tiered differentiated assignment on graphic novels in general and *Maus I* and *Maus II* in particular.

Figure 4–8

Planning Guide: Graphic Novels

Course Title and Level: Grade 9 English
Unit: Graphic Novels

Essential Questions

How can ideas and stories be represented in different modes?
How do different modes of representation affect the reader?
How do schools decide what literature is studied in the classroom?

Unit-Specific Questions

How did graphic novels develop?
What are the pros and cons of using graphic novels in the classroom?

Knowledge/Skills

Students will know how to conduct research.
Students will understand the history of graphic novels.
Students will know how graphic novels are constructed.
Students will understand why graphic novels appeal to adolescents.
Students will understand the pros and cons of using graphic novels in an English class.
Students will be able to present their work in a multimodal form.

Modes of Differentiation Used

Content: differentiate by tiering
Product: differentiate by choice

Based on (readiness, interests, learning styles)

Content: based on readiness
Product: based on interests and learning styles

Figure 4–9

Graphic Novels: Tiering Tasks

Note to teachers: As with any tiering tasks, the teacher needs to decide whether the tiers will be assigned or self-selected. The following are presented in order from basic to advanced learner for planning purposes. They would not be presented to students in this order.

Directions to students: You are going to investigate questions about the history, production, and teaching of graphic novels. When you have completed your investigation, you will present the information to the class in a format that includes a visual. You can choose to present the visual in print or digital form. For example, you may construct a presentation board, create a PowerPoint display, or construct several panels in a graphic novel format.

Tier One

What is a graphic novel? What are its roots? How is a graphic novel similar to and different from a traditional novel? What are different forms of graphic novels? Why do graphic novels appeal to many adolescents?

Tier Two

Why did Art Spiegelman create *Maus I: A Survivor's Story*? Why did he create *Maus II* five years later? How is the portrayal of Holocaust events presented in *Maus I* and *Maus II* similar to and different from the account in a history textbook? What is the Pulitzer Prize and why did Maus win it in 1992?

Tier Three

What are the pros and cons of including graphic novels in an English language arts class? Why might the use of graphic novels in a school be a controversial issue? How does your school decide which texts to include in the English language arts curricula? What do you think should be the future of graphic novels in English language arts classes and why?

A third way teachers are using graphic novels is as writing prompts. Nancy Frey and Douglas Fisher (2007) were looking for a way to connect popular culture in the form of a graphic novel to their writing assignments. They believed that "the limited amount and level of the text would allow students to read and respond to complex messages and text combinations that better matched their reading level" (133). They chose Will Eisner's *New York: The Big City* (1986) for their writing unit. They began by giving students copies of wordless visual panels. As a class, they did a think-aloud and brainstormed descriptive words for the visuals they saw in the panels. Students then wrote their own stories and added words to accompany the drawings. They repeated the process with several other graphic novels. Frey and Fisher found that "visual stories allowed students to discuss how the author conveyed mood and tone through images. They could then discuss techniques for doing so through words" (2007, 135). During their writing unit, the teachers included skill lessons. Frey and Fisher concluded, "Using graphic novels to scaffold writing instruction helped students practice the craft of writing and gain the necessary skills to become competent readers" (142).

The writing unit described by Frey and Fisher offers many opportunities to differentiate instruction. One way to differentiate is to determine which skills students need and to present specific skill instruction to a group of students who seem to have similar needs. For example, students who need sentence combining could meet with the teacher for minilessons and practice that skill, while others continue writing or revising their panels. Another group could then meet with the teacher to review writing dialogue, if that is an area they need to practice. In their article, Frey and Fisher provide a list of graphic novels and picture books used as writing prompts (2007, 135–36). Such a list offers another way to differentiate instruction by asking students to choose the next book they want to read and write about. Finally, more advanced students may create their own graphic novels based on literary works or on their own autobiographies (Schwartz 2002, 5).

Adolescent Literacy, Differentiated Instruction, and Reading

All of the activities and strategies discussed in this chapter are meant as examples and guides for teachers who want to help adolescents use reading to learn more about content and more about themselves as readers, thinkers, learners, and people. The activities and strategies are suggested so that teachers first can determine their own students' interests, readiness, and learning styles and then possibly match their learners to these suggestions. Teachers are encouraged to deviate from, amplify, and further differentiate these activities and strategies.

Writing and
Differentiated Instruction

When adolescents enter middle school and high school, the repertoire of genres they are asked to produce expands to include more expository writing in multiple disciplines. When faced with writing in a new form, such as a comparison essay, even competent writers may backslide at first. They need to be reminded of the strategies they used successfully in the past and be shown new strategies for composing unfamiliar text forms. Today's adolescents are composing longer texts, writing more digitally, and integrating more visuals into their texts. As they face new challenges, teachers need to help adolescent writers understand that the basic process remains the same.

Since the publication of Janet Emig's seminal work *The Composing Processes of Twelfth Graders* (1971), teachers have recognized that writing is a process. During the early seventies, there was a paradigm shift in the teaching of writing from the old model, in which teachers would assign, collect, assess, and return papers, to a new model that allowed time for students to prewrite, draft, revise, edit, and publish their written work. In 2008, The National Council of Teachers of

English (NCTE) published a policy research brief on writing instruction and assessment entitled *Writing Now*. In addition to reinforcing the writing process, this report emphasizes three main dimensions of writing, noting that it needs to be holistic, authentic, and varied. *Holistic* means that writing is viewed as an ongoing process with grammar and mechanics integrated into the whole. *Authentic* means addressing writing in a real-world context by creating assignments that connect to students' lives by providing real audiences and purposes. And *varied* refers not only to differences in the type of texts composed but also to differences in the readiness levels and proficiency of the writers.

In the almost thirty years from the publication of Emig's work to the report from NCTE, we have learned much about all the stages of the writing process, from selecting a topic to editing and publishing a final text. We now take a more holistic approach to this process. We know that although the writing process appears linear, it is actually recursive. When writers focus on drafting a text, for example, they may interrupt the process with editing and then return to drafting. This type of recursive behavior shows the idiosyncratic nature of the writing process, highlighting one of the most important things learned about writing— that it is as unique as each writer. Writers do not move through the process at the same speed, nor do they employ the same strategies even when writing on the same topic and in the same genre. Teachers, therefore, need a repertoire of instructional strategies to address the differences in their students' writing processes. As noted in *Writing Now*, "Research cannot identify one single approach to writing instruction that will be effective with every learner because of diverse backgrounds and learning styles of students who respond differently to various approaches" (NCTE 2008b). This observation was highlighted in the Carnegie Corporation's report, *Writing Next*, published by the Alliance for Excellent Education (Graham and Perin 2007): "In the medical profession, treatment is tailored to individual needs; at times, more than one intervention is needed to effectively treat a patient. Similarly, educators need to test mixes of instruction to find ones that work best for students with different needs" (12). The writers are as varied as the texts they produce. In a differentiated classroom, teachers use an array of instructional strategies to address these differences.

Another important thing teachers learned about writing is that people write better when writing is authentic. Authentic writing focuses on writing assignments that are connected to the world outside the classroom as much as possible. This means that students are offered real purposes and audiences for their writing—for example, writing to persuade the principal to change something in the school or writing to introduce themselves to a college for admission. A second aspect of authentic writing is providing topics that connect to students' interests and concerns. Students produce better written work when they know and care about their topic. As Lucy Calkins (1994) reminds us, "We will tap into an enormous source when we bring students' interests into the classroom" (4). This is why giving students choice is an important part of keeping writing authentic.

One goal of English educators is to help students become independent writers. In order for this to happen, teachers need to give adolescent writers opportunities to make their own choices. They need assignments that provide choice of purpose, topic, audience, and genre. Choice, an important component of differentiated instruction, is based on the students' perceptions of their own readiness levels, personal and academic interests, and learning preferences. When using a process approach to writing, choice can become part of the process at every stage. There are, however, times when teachers need to set parameters for writing assignments, and there may even be times when the whole class is writing on the same topic at the same time for the same amount of time. Timed writing tasks are a necessary part of the total writing experience. Students need to be able to write on a given topic in a timed situation in order to succeed on standardized tests such as state graduation assessments and the Scholastic Assessment Test (SAT). But even on these standardized tests many of the prompts for writing allow room for students to apply the topic to their own personal or academic experiences.

The shift to a process model for teaching writing was the first time many English teachers experienced differentiated instruction in their classrooms. As with other learning experiences, there are three things that can be differentiated when focusing on writing: the process, the content, and the product. The overall writing process provides a model for differentiation because of the decisions a writer needs to make at each stage. In addition, the time frame, the amount and type of instruction, and the timing and type of feedback can all be adjusted to address individual needs. Concerning content, teachers can build an element of choice into the selection of topic, purpose, audience, and genre. The written product can be differentiated by offering students opportunities to write in many different genres. In addition, the written product can be composed in different ways: writing alone, writing with a partner, or writing in a small group. Ways to differentiate content, process, and product can be seen by taking a closer look at each stage of the overall writing process.

Differentiated Instruction and the Writing Process

Although the writing process is holistic and recursive, in order to discuss instructional strategies that can be differentiated and can aid writers at specific points during the composing process, we have presented the stages as a linear model.

Prewriting

During prewriting, students select a topic and identify an audience and purpose for the writing. These decisions are related to the genre or form the writing will take. Personal interest can be an important part of the student's selection of topic. For example, if a student has an interest in surf fishing, he or she may decide to write a piece about fishing rights offshore. The student then needs to decide on the purpose and audience for the writing. If, for example, the writer wants to persuade officials to limit access to certain waters, he or she may choose to write a persuasive piece for the local newspaper, thus clarifying the purpose, audience, and genre.

One of the first steps in prewriting is to brainstorm ideas about a topic, whether the topic is self-selected or assigned. A look at the prewriting a group of three hundred students did on a high-stakes test provides some interesting insights into this part of the writing process. The students were all eleventh graders in a large suburban high school. The test asked the students to write a persuasive essay in response to a given prompt. The test booklet contained a blank sheet that students could use if they wished to prewrite. It was not required. An informal survey found that the majority of students did some form of prewriting, including brainstorming and organizing ideas. The form of their prewriting fell into three categories: listing ideas or topics, writing an informal outline, and creating a graphic organizer such as a web or cluster. The web graphic organizer was the most common form of prewriting found.

When it came to prewriting under timed high-stakes conditions, some students chose not to write anything on the planning page. The students in this group generally fell into two categories: those who scored poorly, below the passing score, and those who scored highly, in the top third of the general school population. Some students are internal planners. The ones who planned successfully throughout the year in their English class did well on the test. The other group of students who did not write anything on the prewriting page tended to write very little on the test and scored very low. These students' writings might have benefited from some form of prewriting, but they chose not to do so.

Prewriting provides a key time to differentiate the process based on student interest or preference. Students need the opportunity to select the prewriting strategy that they prefer and that is successful for them. The teacher can help by giving students multiple opportunities to try different prewriting strategies. Many teachers instruct their students in the use of graphic organizers to plan, to brainstorm ideas, and to begin organizing ideas. Graphic organizers provide a visual representation of ideas and their relationship to each other. Graphic organizers, such as a Venn diagram for a comparison/contrast paper or a character trait chart for a literary analysis essay, are popular in writing classrooms. Teachers and students have also discovered that many of the same graphic organizers used for prewriting (planning what to include in a paper) can be used for postreading (drawing main ideas from a text).

The element of choice is what is important here. This was the main lesson learned from the informal study of prewriting noted earlier. In order to prepare students to be independent writers, we need to teach them various strategies for prewriting and then let them choose the ones they prefer to use, including internal planning. If, however, a strategy a student selects during our class assignments is not successful the teacher needs to be ready to confer with that student and, working together, determine why it failed or whether another prewriting strategy would be more successful. Figure 5–1 is a prewriting choice board for persuasive writing. The choice board in Figure 5–2 includes prewriting and other writing persuasive tasks. Additional prewriting tasks are presented in the strategy section at the end of this chapter.

Figure 5–1

Prewriting Choice Board

Directions for students: Select two revising tasks from the choice board and apply them to a text you are composing. These tasks will be submitted with your final work.

Graphic Organizer	Freewriting	Listing
Create a graphic organizer to arrange and connect your thoughts or use one of the graphic organizers we reviewed in class.	Take a clean piece of paper or a blank computer screen and begin freewriting whatever comes to mind about the topic.	Take a few minutes to think about your topic and then make a list of any ideas that come to mind.
Talk with a Peer	**Free Choice**	**Confer with Your Teacher**
Sometimes it is helpful to talk through your ideas with someone. Find a partner and share your thoughts with each other. It may help to jot down ideas as you talk.	Is there a prewriting strategy that works for you and is not included here? Use that strategy and be ready to explain it.	It may be helpful to talk about your ideas for writing with your teacher, especially if you are stuck. Sign up for a conference.
Review Your Journal or Notes	**Formal or Informal Research**	**Clustering**
Sometimes you store ideas in your journal, writing notebook, or folder. Go back and review some of these. Consider: Can any of these ideas be developed into a writing topic for this assignment?	Sometimes when we are stuck writing, it is because we do not know enough about the topic. It may help to do some research, including rereading related texts that were read in class or at home.	Make a big circle in the middle of a page and write your topic in it. Next, using smaller circles that branch off from the center, jot down related ideas that come to mind, one idea for each circle. Continue clustering connected circles as needed.

Figure 5–2

Persuasive Writing Choice Board

Directions for students: This is a choice board. Everyone must complete the center box. In addition, you are to select and complete two other tasks. You may not select the two tasks from the same row (horizontally). All three tasks will be collected and assessed.

Note to teachers: This can be adapted to be a tic-tac-toe board that requires three tasks be chosen vertically or horizontally, making sure the selections go through the center box.

Complete a graphic organizer on the issue you selected for the center box.	Make a list of pros and cons for the issue you selected for the center box.	Freewrite on the topic you picked for the center box.
Select a persuasive article from a newspaper or periodical and identify the persuasive devices the author used. Label each device.	Write a persuasive essay on a controversial issue you feel is important to teenagers today.	Read a persuasive article in a newspaper or periodical. Identify the audience for the piece. Explain briefly how the article would change if given a different audience.
Create a visual to accompany the essay you are writing for the center box.	Select a persuasive article about a current event. Identify two sides of the argument. Write a brief summary of each side.	Select a print advertisement. Identify and label the persuasive techniques used in the ad. Identify the main audience for this ad.

Drafting

When drafting a piece of writing, the writer is focused on getting ideas down on paper in a logical order. Writers need to be encouraged to write freely without being overly concerned about the mechanics or rules of grammar. Worrying too much about "getting it right" can interfere with the flow of ideas during the drafting stage. Teachers used to think that it was best to leave a student alone during the drafting stage so as not to interrupt the flow of ideas; however, today's teachers realize that some students benefit from intervention during the drafting stage. Lucy Calkins (1994) has identified different forms of conferences that aid writers (see the conferencing section later in this chapter). Some forms of conferencing may be necessary during drafting. If, for example, a student stares too long at a blank page or empty screen, it may help to talk with a teacher or peer about what the writer is trying to accomplish with this paper. At this point in the writing process, the teacher can give various suggestions for getting started, from freewriting to getting up and taking a walk. The strategies for overcoming writer's block can be as varied as the writer. For some students, a little encouragement is all that is needed, while for others, allowing them to talk through their ideas and ask questions may help. Students also prefer different environments for writing. Some students prefer to do most of their writing at home, where they are in a relaxed atmosphere or can have music playing, while other students cannot complete a writing assignment unless they are in a quiet, controlled environment such as a classroom. Teachers need to be aware of these different preferences and create a supportive environment. For example, a student once expressed the need to go into a corner and face the wall when she wrote so that all extraneous outside stimuli were blocked out. She had a classmate, on the other hand, who insisted he couldn't write in school because it was too quiet. Teachers need to establish a classroom environment for writing that allows for differences in the way students move through the writing process. Although there are many constraints in a classroom setting, some variations in the environment can be established.

Teachers can create quiet writing areas by using bookshelves as dividers. In an ideal situation, the classroom would have several carrels such as those found in a library. If neither bookshelves nor carrels are available, a simple quiet writing area can be constructed by facing a couple desks toward a wall in a corner of the room.

In addition, desks can be moved together to form areas for giving and receiving peer feedback. Although musical devices with headphones are not permitted in most classrooms, there are students for whom this may be a necessary learning strategy. This strategy, for example, may be included in individual educational plans for special needs students.

Revising

Over the past thirty years, teachers have become more aware of the importance of revising in the writing process and have learned some key things about it. Revising takes time, leads to multiple drafts, needs to be separated from editing, and is difficult to end. Revising offers many opportunities for differentiation for both the teacher and the students. Teachers can differentiate the instructional practices they use to teach revision. Students can differentiate the strategies they use to revise.

Although they are in middle school and high school, adolescent writers continue to need instruction and practice revising their written work. They may know some general revision strategies, but when confronted with more challenging writing tasks, their previous methods for revising may not work, or they may need to be reminded how and when to employ revision strategies. As with all forms of differentiated instruction, teachers need to begin with preassessment. At the beginning of the school year, it is useful to survey students either formally or informally to ascertain what revising practices they use. Teachers can also observe students when they are revising in the classroom. Based on the information collected, the teacher can then decide which revision strategies need to be taught or reviewed as a whole class and which students need more individual or small-group instruction in the revising process. The revision strategies listed here cover a range of learning styles.

- Let the paper sit overnight, then revise it.

- Read the paper aloud to yourself.

- Have a peer read the paper aloud to you.

- Join a peer feedback group.

- Highlight parts of the paper you think need revising.

- Using different-colored highlighters for each main idea, trace each main idea from the introduction through the paper.

- Circle all transitions between ideas.

- Cut and paste parts of your paper to reorder ideas.

- Create a "holding bin" for ideas that need to be eliminated because they do not fit here and now.

Teachers can create tasks to help students practice different revising strategies. As students become more familiar with different forms of revision, they can choose ones that work well for them. Figure 5–3 is a choice board that contains a variety of revision tasks.

Editing

Although the writing process is holistic, there is a point at which the writer needs to read the composition with an eye toward editing. Because editing is often confused with revision, it is important to take the time to reinforce the difference with students. When revising, the author is addressing the deep structure of a piece—its content and organization. When the focus is on editing, the author is addressing the surface issues of grammar, usage, mechanics, and spelling. Sentence structure sits on the fence between revision and editing. Sentences can be evaluated based on their meaning in the piece and how they link ideas. In this case, they are part of the revision process. But when the focus is on the surface level of sentence structure, such as run-ons and sentence fragments, the sentences are evaluated during the editing stage. It is, however, important to remember that the writing stages are not always sequential. The writing process is actually recursive, and the writer can stop at any time and revisit a previous stage. Editing can often interrupt the flow of ideas when a student is drafting or revising. Students may jot down editing concerns when this happens or edit briefly so that it does not interrupt the drafting or revising for very long.

Instruction in editing can range from direct instruction in grammar and mechanics to practice editing peer papers. Figure 5–4 presents differentiated stations for students to rotate through as they practice editing skills.

Figure 5–3

Revising Choice Board

Directions for students: Select three revising tasks from the choice board and apply them to a text you are composing.

Peer Revising	Personal Checklist	Main Ideas and Support
Find a peer who is also working on revising a paper and take turns giving revision suggestions. Remember to read the papers through before offering suggestions.	Take out the personal revising checklist that you created for your writing folder. Check your present paper against the suggestions for changes made in the past.	Take a hard copy of your text and, using different-colored highlighters, trace each main point and its support throughout your paper.
Cut and Paste	**Free Choice**	**Transitions**
Sometimes it is necessary to rearrange your ideas, delete ideas, or add new ideas. This can be done by either cutting and pasting your writing on a computer screen or doing so with a hard copy. Reread your draft after cutting and pasting.	You are the author of your paper. Others can make suggestions for change, but you decide what to write and how to write it. If you have a strategy for revising that works for you, apply it to your paper. Be ready to explain your revising process.	During the revising process, check to see if you have included transitions between ideas. Also check to see if you used different transitions and that they fit your meaning.
Leave It Alone	**Openings and Closings**	**Teacher Conference**
Sometimes during the revising process, you need to leave your paper alone for a while. Get up, take a walk, stretch, or maybe get a drink of water. Do something different for a while and then return to your revising.	Either alone or with a peer, reread your introduction and your conclusion. Do they accomplish their purposes? Is there a better way to begin your paper? Is the ending clear and final? Make any changes needed.	Decide if it is time to discuss your revisions with your teacher. Think about questions you want to ask. Be ready to explain any changes you are making. (Your teacher may also request the conference.)

Figure 5–4

Skills Stations: Editing

These stations are to be completed during a ninety-minute class block. If a class runs forty-five minutes, the stations can be completed over two class periods.

Directions when there is free choice: Today you will be completing three out of the five editing stations presented. Everyone is required to complete station five. You may select the other two stations you wish to complete. The stations can be completed in any order. Please keep track of the time. Your completed work should be placed into your folder. The folder will be collected at the end of class.

Directions when task cards are used to assign stations: Read the task cards in your folder and complete the stations listed on those cards. You may complete them in any order. Please keep track of the time. Your completed work should be placed into your folder. The folder will be collected at the end of class.

Station One

Sentence combining: Take the worksheet and follow the instructions to combine the sentences in each section.

Station Two

Read the paragraphs provided and edit them for grammar, usage, mechanics, and spelling (G.U.M.S.).

Station Three

Read this excerpt from a magazine article. Using a highlighter provided, highlight as many commas as you can identify in the excerpt. Next, write the reason for the journalist's use of each comma.

Station Four

Finding a better word: Read the paragraphs provided, paying close attention to the highlighted words or phrases. Think of a better way to state the word or phrase highlighted. Write your revisions at the bottom of the sheet.

Station Five

Take a draft of the paper you are working on out of your folder. Read it carefully and circle any errors you see in G.U.M.S. You may begin correcting them as time permits. If you have any questions about editing changes, sign up to meet with the teacher. If you see no errors or have no questions about the G.U.M.S. in your paper and you have time left, you may help a classmate edit his or her paper.

By the time adolescents reach middle school and high school, often there is a wide discrepancy in their understanding of grammar and, more importantly, in their ability to apply it correctly in writing. We do not believe that students need to memorize grammatical rules and be able to reference them on a quiz or test. Students do need to use correct grammatical concepts in their writing in order to communicate their ideas clearly. Because there is a wide range of competence in this area of writing, teachers often differentiate direct instruction when addressing grammatical concerns. The choice board in Figure 5–5 contains differentiated grammar tasks based on multiple intelligences. Each task gives students the opportunity to review and practice grammatical concepts in a style they are most comfortable with.

Publishing

Publishing gives student writers a true sense of audience. When students know a piece of writing will be read by others, they are more likely to give it their best efforts. There are many informal and formal publishing opportunities for adolescent writers. Informal publishing opportunities are found within the classroom or school building. These range from reading the text aloud to a peer or to the whole class to posting the piece on a schoolwide bulletin board. Using electronic sources in the school, a student text may be posted on a website or wiki. Outside the school environment, there are almost limitless possibilities for more formal publication. These range from entering a writing contest to posting the work on a blog. Differentiation is important at this stage because we have found that some students are more comfortable with sharing their work than others. We need to be prepared to offer alternatives to public publication such as a more private teacher-student reading basis. An assignment that motivates many student writers is to have them research publication opportunities for teens, either working alone or in small groups. We begin by suggesting two traditional resources such as the NCTE and the Scholastic writing competitions and then have them explore other print and electronic sources for publication. The school librarian or media specialist is a good resource for helping students initiate a search.

Figure 5–5

Grammar and Multiple Intelligences Choice Board

Directions for students: Select two tasks from the choice board.

Musical	Naturalistic	Linguistic/Verbal
Select three grammar rules and set them to music, sing them, or create a rap for them. Perform these for the class.	As a botanist observing the growth of a plant, write a one-page report of the growth you observe using correct punctuation and a version without punctuation. Give the one without punctuation to a classmate to read. Then ask him or her to add punctuation where it belongs. Compare this version to your punctuated version.	Select three basic grammar rules. Tell the class how you would explain them to a fourth grader. Then write out the explanation.
Logical/Mathematical	**Free Choice Square**	**Bodily/Kinesthetic**
Review the last three papers you wrote. Using graph paper, chart your grammatical errors. Analyze the chart. Were any errors repeated? What does this chart show you?	Suggest your own task. It may represent any of the eight intelligences or it may be a combination.	Work with others in your class to create a punctuation performance. After you write a paragraph on a topic of your choice, you and your classmates become punctuation symbols and insert yourselves into the text as it is read orally to the class.
Intrapersonal	**Spatial**	**Interpersonal**
Write a journal entry in which you reflect on how correct grammar helps you to think and to communicate.	Create a board or electronic game in which students have to place the correct punctuation in order to win.	Prepare an oral presentation to persuade the class that adhering to grammatical rules is important for interpersonal communication.

Differentiated Instruction and Conferencing

Receiving feedback is critical to improving writing. Formative feedback can be given during the composing of a text, and summative feedback can be given on the final product. Chapter 3 in this book discusses these two types of feedback as they relate to adolescent literacy. In writing instruction, feedback during the composing process is most often given in the form of conferences. Conferencing, discussing a piece of writing with its author, is a familiar differentiated practice; by its very nature, a conference differentiates instruction by focusing on an individual, unique piece of writing produced by one student. Conferencing, an integral part of the writing workshop classroom model, can occur at any stage of the writing process and can be conducted by the teacher or by peers.

Calkins (1994) offers a useful model for identifying different types of conferences teachers and peers have with student writers: content, design, process, and evaluation conferences. Content conferences focus on selecting the topic and discussing what the writer wants to say about it. Design conferences focus on clarifying the form or genre for the piece of writing, maintaining the purpose for writing, and checking the organization of the piece. Process conferences focus on the writer's experiences during the writing process. Evaluation conferences focus on assessment of the written work by the writer, the teacher, or peers. These different types of conferences can be built into the writing process. Content conferences are held when a writer is prewriting, planning a topic. Design conferences are held during the prewriting or early drafting stages of producing a piece. Process conferences can be held at any stage or at the end of the writing process. Process conferences can focus on one stage, such as prewriting or revising, or they can address the whole writing process from prewriting to publishing.

Writing conferences can also be differentiated by who initiates the conference. The student or the teacher can ask for a conference. Students generally initiate conferences when they are stumped—for example, when they have a problem with writing an ending to their paper or when they don't know how to punctuate a challenging sentence. Teachers may initiate conferences on a regularly scheduled basis or they may call for a conference when they see a need. Giving students the opportunity to decide when and how to conference reinforces their ownership of the writing process. Talking with students about their writing processes and observing them at every stage are the best ways for teachers to decide when and how to differentiate instruction.

Differentiating Using Writing Folders and Portfolios

Writing folders and writing portfolios provide another opportunity for students to take ownership of their learning. There is a difference between a writing folder and a writing portfolio. Some teachers do not distinguish between writing folders and portfolios, using the terms interchangeably; however, no matter what term is used, the folder or portfolio belongs to the student, and the student makes decisions about what goes into it.

A portfolio is a place to collect and display selected work samples and reflections. A writing folder contains works in progress, writing ideas, and checklists. It is a place where students can keep ideas for and drafts of their writing. It may also include personal editing and revising checklists. Writing folders are unique to each learner and, therefore, differentiated.

Even when students are working on the same writing assignment and topic, their work is individualized. Revising and editing checklists can be differentiated to fit the needs of each student based on past performance in writing. When working with adolescent writers, teachers need to encourage students to be responsible for keeping and updating their personal revising and editing records. When a writing assignment is returned, before filing the completed work in a folder or portfolio, students should read over the comments and suggestions their peers or teacher have made and record them on their personal revising or editing lists.

A portfolio, unlike a writing folder, does not include everything that has been written. A portfolio that contains the pieces the writer is most proud of or pieces that show the greatest improvement is referred to as a "best works" or "showcase" portfolio. To create this type of portfolio, students need to collect, select, and reflect on their writing samples.

Collection of potential portfolio pieces occurs in the writing folder. The writing folder contains all drafts and works in progress as well as finished pieces. From this collection of work, a student selects the writing samples he or she wishes to include in the showcase portfolio. The selection of writing samples may be done by the student alone or by the student in consultation with the teacher. Some teachers ask students to select a certain number of pieces and also reserve the right to add another piece. The pieces in a showcase portfolio represent the best work the student has completed during the time period covered by the portfolio. A variation on the showcase portfolio is a progress or growth portfolio. For a progress portfolio, the student selects work that shows improvement over the time frame covered. Both types of portfolios contain work samples collected over time.

After work samples have been collected and selected for inclusion in the portfolio, the student reflects on the choices. Reflection is key because it prompts students to self-evaluate the work they have been doing and to plan for future work. Teachers often provide prompts to help reflect on their work. These prompts may be differentiated based on the purpose of the portfolio and individual student needs. The reflection for a showcase portfolio might focus on how the writing sample represents the student's best work, while the reflection for a progress portfolio might focus on how a writing sample shows improvement over previous work. The following list of reflection prompts can be adapted for both types of portfolios.

- Why did I select this piece of writing?

- How does this represent my best work?

- Why am I proud of this piece of writing?

- What did I learn by writing this piece?

- How does this piece show improvement over my previous writing?

- What do I need to work on next in my writing?

- What type of help do I need to continue to improve?

Electronic or digital portfolios are becoming more common. The problems of storage and maintenance of portfolios have helped to make digital portfolios more popular in a school setting. At one suburban high school, the storing of best works portfolios grew from one small closet off the media center to two large storage closets on two floors. Just keeping track of which grade-level portfolios were stored on which floor and in what order became a challenge. When it was time to store or retrieve student work, a master list had to be consulted.

Technology offers an alternative to paper-based portfolios. Digital portfolios can include digital photos, videos, and sound elements in addition to written texts. To make it easier to maintain the portfolios, they can be burned onto individual CD-ROMs. A potential problem for keeping digital portfolios is the occasional failure of software or the mistaken erasure of work completed. Although they are not risk-free, some schools are finding digital portfolios much easier to maintain than paper-based ones.

Work folders and portfolios, whether paper or digital, provide evidence of the unique nature of writing and learning to write. The teacher and student can hold a conference to discuss the contents of the portfolio and to review the student's reasons for making the choices for the selection. This conference can become part of the formative or summative assessment process. By allowing the student to decide on the content of the portfolio and to lead the discussion during the conference, teachers can differentiate the type and amount of feedback given to each student.

Writing and Differentiating Technology

When computers were first introduced into the English classroom in the late 1970s, teachers were quick to see their use as a tool for writing. The ease with which text could be manipulated using a word-processing program released students from the drudgery of physically rewriting a whole paper when making a revision. Students showed that they were more willing to revise and edit when they used a word-processing program. In addition, they were more willing to produce longer texts. Technology has moved well beyond those early word-processing programs to include writing to and receiving feedback from distant audiences and integrating multiple visuals into a written product. Sara Kajder (2007) reminds us that writing no longer takes place with pen and paper but with a mouse and screen. In more and more classrooms, students compose right on laptop computers. Certainly, most students compose on computers when they write at home. In the not too distant future, our students may even compose longer texts on cell phones.

In Japan, novels produced by composing on cell phones are becoming quite popular. According to Dyna Goodyear (2008), writing in *The New Yorker*, "The cell-phone, or *keitai shosetsu*, is the first literary genre to emerge from the cellular age; . . . the medium—unfiltered, unedited—is revolutionary, opening the closed ranks of the literary world to anyone who owns a mobile phone" (63). One young cell phone novelist who goes by the name of "Rin" explains why cell phone novels are popular with her generation: "They don't read works by professional writers because their sentences are often too difficult to understand, their expressions are intentionally wordy, and the stories are not familiar to them" (Onishi 2008, 1). The cell phone novels are one example of how technology is changing a genre. Novels written on a cell phone contain simpler vocabularies and shorter sentences. Because of their popularity in Japan, cell phone novels may soon become more common in the United States.

Another form of writing gaining in popularity is digital storytelling, personal tales that ordinary people, not professional authors, are sharing using digital tools. Digital storytelling has grown out the tradition of oral storytelling. Digital stories are relatively short (two to four minutes) and may include sound and graphics. The Center for Digital Storytelling has developed a model that can be used by teachers (available at www.storycenter.org). Faculty members at the University of Houston have also developed a website for educational uses of digital storytelling (see http://coe.uh.edu/digitalstorytelling/). In the classroom, digital stories can be integrated into a unit on memoir writing, adding a multimodal element.

Whether they are writing with pen and paper, computers, or even cell phones, the ways our students compose are varied. Teachers need to pay attention not only to the texts their students are producing, but also to the tools they are using. The new technology may not yet be in our classrooms, but it affects what will be happening in our classrooms in the future.

Later in Chapter 8, we address many new technologies and their relationship to adolescent literacy in more depth. It is important to note here that the new digital technologies appeal to different students to different degrees. Not all students are ready to jump on the technology bandwagon, nor do they all have the same access to or fluency with the new technologies. Therefore, teachers need to differentiate for technology and writing the same way we differentiate other teaching and learning tools. Teachers need to preassess to determine both interest in and familiarity with the new technologies that are available for writers. For example, just because it is popular, not all teenagers are comfortable with or prefer to write on a blog. If teachers make technology a requirement for any assignments, they need to make sure the technology is available for all students and that the students are comfortable with it. Finally, teachers need to be prepared to offer instruction on the technology for those students who may need it.

The Writing Process and Anchor Activities

In a classroom in which students are composing different pieces and finishing at different times, anchor activities—purposeful tasks that students can work on and return to when they finish another assignment—are a necessary part of the classroom procedures. Students should keep a list of writing anchor activities in their work folders for those times when they complete their work early and their teacher hasn't assign a specific anchor activity to return to. When suggesting free choice anchor activities, teachers should include activities that appeal to different learning styles. The following is a list of suggested writing anchor activities.

- Write a reflection on the writing you completed today, explaining what worked well for you and what was a challenge.
- Sign up to help a peer revise or edit.
- Revise or edit a piece from your writing folder.
- Check your introduction. Try another way to begin your paper.
- Check your conclusion. Try another way to end your paper.
- Work on an ongoing long-term project.
- Write in your journal.
- Make a list of topics you would like to write about.
- Read a story, essay, or poem that is in a style you would like to write.
- Create a visual to accompany a piece you wrote.
- Take a description from a favorite reading and rewrite it as a poem.
- Write four questions about writing you would like to ask the teacher.

Differentiated Strategies and Writing

The following section presents examples of writing tasks using strategies that support differentiated instruction.

Tiered Assignments

Tiered assignments are based on differences in readiness levels. The goals, the enduring understandings, and the essential questions remain the same, but the level of complexity of the tasks varies. Students who demonstrate an advanced knowledge of the concept or skill being addressed can be asked to complete tasks at a higher level of complexity or abstraction. Students who struggle to learn the basics can be asked to complete a less complex and more concrete task. The following are examples of tiered assignments for persuasive writing and literature writing tasks.

Tiered Persuasive Writing Tasks

Tier 1: Write a letter to your principal convincing her that a rule in your school should be changed.

Tier 2: Write a letter that you will send to the local newspaper stating your opinion on a controversial issue in your town.

Tier 3: Choose a current controversial topic that is in the news and write a persuasive essay presenting your point of view.

Tiered Literature Writing Tasks

Tier 1: Write a character sketch for the main character in the text you read.

Tier 2: Write a literary analysis essay of the antagonist in the text you read.

Tier 3: Write an essay comparing the antagonist in the text you read to a character in another major literary work.

The persuasive writing tasks move from a familiar audience and familiar form to a more distant audience and a more formal format. The writing about literature tasks move from a basic character sketch of one character to a comparison of two characters from different literary works.

Stations

Stations can be based on readiness, interests, learning styles, or any combination of the three. Learning stations differ from learning centers in that they are created for a particular assignment or unit of study and are not permanent work areas in the classroom. Students may have free choice in selecting stations or the stations may be assigned. The classroom teacher differentiates stations by deciding how much choice to allow and which stations to require. Some students have specific directions for completing stations based on the teacher's assessment of their readiness levels. Generally, not all stations are required for every student and may be set up for one or more days. Stations may be differentiated by giving each student a separate list of stations and directions for completing them. Student work from each station is placed into a work folder, which students use to help them as they write, revise, and edit a persuasive paper. Figure 5–6 presents stations for persuasive prewriting.

As adolescents face new challenges in writing, they will be successful if they have developed a solid understanding of the writing process and how to apply it to different forms of writing, including digitally composed texts.

Figure 5–6

Persuasive Prewriting Stations

Station One: Stumped for a Topic?

Choice A: Look through the suggested topics in this folder. Then brainstorm your ideas on one of the topics.

Choice B: Begin your freewriting by finishing this thought, "I would like to convince people that . . ."

Station Two: Responding to Reading

Read the article in the folder and make a list of which parts you agree with and which parts you disagree with. Next, think about which side of the argument you would take if you decide to write about this topic.

Station Three: Point Counterpoint

Once you have decided on a persuasive topic, make a graphic organizer and list all the points you agree with on one side and the points you disagree with on the other side. Read over your lists and decide which side you would support.

Station Four: A Little Help from My Friends

Sometimes talking it through helps to clarify your ideas. If you would like to speak with a peer about your topic, sit at this station and put one of the cards labeled "Let's Talk" in front of you. If you choose this option, you need to focus your talk on the topic for your paper, talk in a quiet voice, and spend no more than ten minutes here. If no peer is ready to talk with you, you may want to move to the consultation station with the teacher.

Station Five: Consultation Station

You will find the teacher at this station. If you have tried to find a topic or have begun writing and are still stumped, you may sign up for a time slot to talk with the teacher.

Station Six: A Picture Can Be Worth a Thousand Words

Having trouble thinking of a good persuasive topic? Look at the pictures in this folder depicting events and situations from our community and around the world. Study a picture and decide what issues it presents.

Speaking, Listening, and Differentiated Instruction

6

Successful communication skills are necessary both inside and outside the classroom, and successful communication depends upon effective speaking and listening skills. In the classroom, students and teachers speak and listen more than they read and write, but as Robert Probst (2007) notes, "We expect [speaking skills], and we do depend on it, but we don't teach it" (45). The same could be said of listening, and most English language arts teachers often neglect to teach these literacies directly. This chapter addresses both speaking and listening because, although all the language arts literacies are interrelated, speaking and listening depend most on each other. Speaking and listening in the English language arts classroom can be approached in two ways: as independent topics to be studied as ends in themselves or as supports for the other literacies of reading, writing, and viewing. For example, students may study the components of good public speaking and then give a formal speech, or they may discuss a character with their peers when meeting in literature circles. In the first example, speech and listening are taught as independent subjects, and in the second example, they are used to support the students' understanding of literature. The first part of this chapter addresses speaking and listening in formal public speaking situations. The second part of the chapter addresses more informal uses for speaking and listening in the classroom.

In order to be successful in speaking, formally or informally, students need to know the purpose and audience for the communication. Purposes for speaking are similar to those for writing: to inform, to persuade, to question, to problem solve, or to entertain. Figure 6–1 offers a list of the most common speaking activities included in English language arts classrooms. Audiences for speaking range from classmates to the general public, depending on the purpose of the speaking task. Teachers need to create an environment and construct lessons that offer different levels of formality in speaking.

Figure 6–1

Common Speaking Activities in Middle and Secondary Schools

author's chair	giving directions	persuasive speech
book reports/talks	impromptu speech	read-alouds
campaign speech	informative speech	read speech
choral reading	interview	reader's theatre
cooperative groups	literary discussion groups	school TV news report
debate	literature circles	Socratic Seminars
dramatic reading	memorized speech	storytelling
enact story/play scenes	oral interpretation of a poem	summaries
entertaining speech	oral sports reporting	think-alouds
extemporaneous speech	peer writing groups	think-pair-share

Formal Speech: Public Speaking and Differentiated Instruction

Most people engage in formal public speaking at some time in their lives. Whether it is presenting a report at a business meeting, presenting oneself at a job interview, or giving a toast at a wedding, there are occasions when the speaker needs to pay attention not only to what is said but also to how it is said. In middle and secondary English language arts classrooms, public speaking can be integrated into a literary or thematic unit that includes a formal presentation or it can be presented as a separate unit of study.

There are several types of formal speeches: extemporaneous, read, impromptu, and memorized. Extemporaneous speeches are the most common formal presentations. They are speeches that are planned, but not written down. A speaker may make an outline of ideas ahead of time but does not have to adhere to it. When presenting an extemporaneous speech, a speaker can respond to the audience and adjust the speech accordingly. Oral reports to the class and campaign speeches are examples of extemporaneous speeches. There are times when a speaker reads the entire speech from a written text. An example of this is when a politician begins a press conference by saying, "I am going to read from a prepared statement." Another example is when a student television reporter reads the daily announcements from a teleprompter. Impromptu speeches are given at a moment's notice. At a student council meeting, for example, a student may be called upon to speak on an issue raised at the meeting. A memorized speech is rarely given. A student may memorize an opening statement in a debate before moving on to present arguments extemporaneously. All forms of formal speeches have the same components: an opening or hook, an organized and logically developed middle, and a definite conclusion. Several elements are necessary for a successful public speaking presentation; a speaker needs to:

- be enthusiastic about the topic
- know the subject

- be clear on the purpose

- consider the audience

- prepare the content

- have an engaging opening

- enunciate clearly

- be well organized

- use appropriate and varied language

- maintain eye contact

- use appropriate gestures

- project the voice

- maintain a conversational pace

- maintain good posture

- integrate visuals as needed

- present a solid conclusion

One of the best ways to become a competent public speaker is to watch and listen to good oratorical examples. Teachers can find examples of famous speeches by searching on the Internet or by consulting their school librarian or media specialist. A website for American Rhetoric, for example, contains what that association considers to be the top 100 speeches of the twentieth century at www.american rhetoric.com/top100speechesall.html. The speeches on this site can be downloaded to an MP3 player. Another website, www.learnoutloud.com, has speeches presented as podcasts and videos. Blogs on famous speeches can also be accessed at www.blogcatalog.com/blogsearch/famous+speeches. The daily news media, electronic and print, are additional sources for current speeches and debates. Election years, for example, offer almost daily examples of public speaking on the local and national levels. As students watch and listen to speeches, they are not only reinforcing what makes a good speaker but also developing effective listening skills.

Differentiating Formal Speeches

When teaching public speaking, teachers can differentiate content, process, and product. Concerning content, although the form of the speech—informative, persuasive, or entertaining—may be required, the topic can be chosen by the student based on interest. Just as with writing, speakers deliver more effective speeches when they care about and know their topics. Students can also select any visual aids they want to incorporate into the oral presentation. In a classroom presentation, the student may also role-play and identify a particular audience for the speech. As noted earlier, differentiating instruction begins with preassessment. A preassessment of readiness levels may reveal that students need help with different aspects of public speaking. The results of the preassessment can help teachers differentiate the process by varying the type and amount of instructional support the teacher provides. Some students are reluctant public speakers and may need more positive reinforcement and more practice sessions than their peers. On the other hand, students who are very comfortable speaking publicly may need help in organizing their ideas for presentation. Although the product is often clearly identified in a speaking unit, such as giving an informative speech, the teacher can differentiate the product by altering the length of the speeches or by allowing students to present their speeches to different audiences.

After a general introduction to public speaking, teachers can work with small groups or individual students based on their needs. While the teacher meets with small groups of students, the rest of the class can be working on researching their topics and preparing their speeches. Figure 6–2 is a choice board that presents speaking and listening activities that are differentiated by student interests and readiness levels. The following section presents selected formal speaking classroom activities.

Formal Speaking Classroom Activities

Persuasive Speech

Persuasive speeches are often included in English language arts curricula. The object of a persuasive speech is to convince an audience to agree with the

Figure 6–2

Speaking and Listening Choice Board

Directions for students: Select three tasks to complete—one from the first row, one from the second row, and one from the third row.

Note to teachers: Some teachers make this a menu board by labeling the first row *appetizer*, the second row *entrée*, and the third row *dessert*. Students are then instructed to pick one appetizer, one entrée, and one dessert.

Watch a national television news program. Keep a log and identify any elements of good speaking employed by the news anchor and reporters. Be ready to explain your findings.	Watch your school or local television news. Keep a log and record what you feel is effective and what you feel needs improvement. Be ready to send your observations to the program's director.	Watch a weekend news program that includes interviewing guests. What can you learn from this show about effective questioning and listening skills? Be ready to present your observations to the class.
Listen to a radio program that contains mainly people speaking, for example, shows on public radio. Keep a log and record examples of speech that are effective and explain why.	Listen to a class lecture or presentation and take notes. Wait a day and reread your notes. How clear are they? Is there anything you missed? How would you change the way you take notes to make the process more effective?	When you are eating lunch or otherwise engaged with a group of peers, listen carefully to the conversation. Can you tell when others are listening carefully? Can you tell when they are not? What advice can you give your peers about participating in a conversation?
Select a topic you want to present to the class in an oral presentation. Research the topic, plan a speech, and be ready to present it to the class.	Create a video or a podcast of a speech you have prepared and present it to the class.	Select an adult in your school that you would like to interview. Prepare the interview questions, make an appointment, and interview that person. Present your findings orally to the class.

speaker's point of view or stand on an issue. Persuasive speeches may be part of a unit on persuasion that also includes writing and viewing, as these media use many of the same persuasive devices, such as those listed in Chapter 7 (Figure 7–5, p. 110). The first step in preparing and delivering a persuasive speech is to decide on a topic. Carousel brainstorming, an activity that actively engages students, helps students identify and select a persuasive topic. The teacher posts large sheets of blank paper around the room and places a controversial topic at the top of each sheet, forming carousel stations around the room. The students are divided into groups of four to six participants, and each group chooses a recorder. The recorder for each group is given a different-colored marker. As the groups move from station to station, the recorder writes the group's ideas directly onto the posted paper. By giving each group a different-colored marker, the teacher and students can easily see which comments each group made. The statements posted at the top of the sheets need to be controversial, forcing each group to take a stand: for example, "Community service should be a requirement for graduation from high school." Each group reads the statement, discusses it, and then writes down the group's views on the posted topic. Each group can write as many comments as the time allows. When time is called, each group rotates to the next station. The students read what the previous groups have written on the sheets of paper, putting a check mark next to any statements they agree with before adding new comments. This process continues until each group is back at its starting place. The teacher then calls for quiet time, and the students walk silently around the room, read what has been written, and return to their seats. When this has been completed, the teacher explains that the students can choose one of the brainstormed topics for their persuasive speeches or suggest other topics. The benefits of choosing one of the carousel brainstorming topics is that many points the speaker may want to include have already been identified. The sheets of paper are left up for several days for the students to consult.

After deciding on a topic, the next thing a speaker needs to do is identify the audience and purpose for the talk. In the example of community service, the student speaker needs to decide if the audience is classmates, parents, or school administrators. The speaker must also decide which side of the argument to take. Once the audience and stand are clearly identified, the purpose becomes clearer.

For example, if the audience for the community service topic is school adminis-trators and the speaker takes a stand against this requirement, the purpose of the speech is to convince the administrators that they should not make community service a graduation requirement.

After identifying the topic, audience, and purpose for the speech, the speaker concentrates on content and organization. Preparing the content often includes conducting some research so that the presentation is based on facts as well as opinions. Arguments in speeches are based on evidence that includes facts, statis-tics, anecdotes, and expert opinions. Both sides of the argument need to be weighed so that opposing arguments can be addressed and answered. Once the research is completed, the notes have to be organized so that the arguments are presented in a logical order. Student speakers need to organize their points or itemize their contentions in much the same way they organize an essay. Opening remarks and conclusions are especially important to draw the audience in and to leave the audience with a clear message. If any visual aids are going to be integrated into the speech, their use needs to be highlighted in the notes. Finally, a speaker needs to rehearse the presentation, timing it and making any necessary changes. It is often helpful to have a practice audience and to record the practice sessions so that the speakers can hear themselves. The steps for preparing and delivering a persuasive speech outlined here apply to other forms of formal speeches, including speeches to inform, to commemorate, and to entertain.

Debate

A debate is an argument presented by two or more people, following prescribed rules. The debate format in schools typically has two teams presenting opposing sides of an argument that is presented as a resolution. In many parts of the country, school debates have become an interscholastic competition. For many years, studying debate was a required part of secondary English curricula. Debate no longer has the prominence it once did. In some schools, it is offered only as an elective or an after-school club. There are good reasons for including debate in the English language arts curriculum. According to Kate Shuster (2006), author of a number of debate books and administrator of a debate website (www.middleschooldebate.com), the many benefits to teaching debate include building research competence, media literacy, reading comprehension, argument literacy, evidence evaluation, summarization, outlining, public speaking, conflict resolution, civil discussion, critical thinking, and note taking.

For those teachers uncomfortable teaching debate because they have little training in it, debate models and lessons can be found in textbooks and online by searching for "teaching debate" or "formal debate." A good starting point is to do a Web search for "The National High School Debate Topic." Many schools have debate websites linked to this site. Additional information on debates can be found at the website for the International Debate Education Association at www.idebate.org. Middle school teachers can consult the Middle School Public Debate Program at http://middleschooldebate.com. Secondary teachers can find information on debate competitions at www.americanforensics.org/hischool.html.

Students studying debate need to be familiar with the format of debates and how they will be judged. There are several different formal debate models. Figure 6–3 presents one traditional high school debate format. It does not include cross-examination, as this is a more advanced skill. However, when differentiating instruction for debate, some students may be ready to research and practice a cross-examination model.

To become more familiar with debate formats, debate judging, and debate strategies, students can be assigned different topics to research. The assignment in Figure 6–4 presents a range of topics for research on debate; the tasks can be self-selected based on interests or assigned based on readiness levels.

Listening is a critical part of any debate. In order for each team to present a rebuttal, team members have to know the arguments presented by their opponent and how to address specific issues or evidence introduced by the opposing team. Debaters listen and take notes when their opponents are speaking. In addition, audience members or classmates can be included in the debate by asking them to take notes and score the speeches. Audience members should be reminded to listen with open minds so that they can judge the speakers on their delivery and content, not on a preconceived opinion about the topic. Student debaters can also do a self-assessment at the end of a debate.

As with other literacy practices, it is helpful for students to see a rubric or scoring guide when the debate is assigned so they know what is expected of them. Classmates in the audience can have copies of the rubric to assess and provide feedback for their peers. Examples of rubrics can be found online at the debate

Figure 6–3

Formal Debate Format: One Model

A formal debate consists of two teams, with three to four members on each team. The length of time for each section varies depending on the grade level of the students or on the debate format used. A range of times is included below.

Proposition: The stated solution to a problem.

Example from The National High School Debate Topic for 2008–2009

Resolved: The United States federal government should substantially increase alternative energy incentives in the United States.

Affirmative: The debaters arguing for the proposition.

Negative: The debaters arguing against the proposition.

Argument: Facts and opinions presented as evidence to support each side's stand.

Constructive speeches: Speeches in which each debater lays out his or her arguments.

Rebuttal speeches: Speeches in which each debater has a chance to refute the opponent's arguments.

Order of speeches:

    Constructive speeches (5–8 minutes)

        First affirmative

        First negative

        Second affirmative

        Second negative

    Rebuttal speeches (3–5 minutes)

        First negative

        First affirmative

        Second negative

        Second affirmative

Figure 6–4

Debate Research

Directions: Your class is going to publish a reference booklet on debate that can be used by other students. Working in groups of four to six students, you will research one of the following topics and then collaboratively write a section on your topic for the debate booklet. Please indicate your first and second choices of topics from the list below. Every effort will be made to assign you to one of your two choices.

- annotated debate terms
- different forms of formal debate
- how debates are judged
- strategies for presenting an argument
- strategies for presenting a rebuttal
- debate advice: what to do and what not to do in debates
- graphic organizers and other ways to plan a debate presentation
- a comparison of two debate evaluation forms
- debate competitions for middle and secondary school students

websites noted earlier in this chapter and at assessment websites, such as www.rubistar4teachers.com. Student audience members can have a copy of the rubric in front of them as they listen to the debate and use the rubric to give feedback to their peers. Anna Roseboro, an award-winning debate coach who teaches speech at Calvin College in Grand Rapids, Michigan, suggests that teachers can create their own feedback forms. Roseboro uses a form she created and requires her students to complete the form anonymously whenever classmates give prepared speeches. She collects the forms, reads them, and, after discarding any that may be hurtful, returns them to the speakers. Giving audience members the task of providing feedback after the debate is a way to reinforce active listening.

Differentiating Debates

Teachers can differentiate participation in debates not only by giving students choice of topic, but also by assigning students different roles in the debate. Students who are good listeners and who can think fast on their feet, for example, would be good rebuttal speakers. Students who plan well and are logical in organizing their thoughts would be effective as constructive speakers, who introduce and present the arguments. In addition, a teacher may need to differentiate the process by giving some students more time to observe debates before they are ready to participate in one.

Interviews

Most jobs require some form of oral communication skills. Even in today's digital world, employers want to meet job applicants in a face-to-face interview. Many colleges also require personal interviews as part of the application process. In order to be prepared for an interview, the applicant needs to obtain information about the company or school. Therefore, the interview process should include researching the company or school conducting the interview.

The person being interviewed has to be a good listener as well as a competent speaker. During an interview, the applicant needs to be able to speak clearly, correctly, and concisely. Clearly means that the speaker needs to articulate words and to speak in a voice that is loud enough to hear in a conversational setting. Correctly means that the speaker needs to use appropriate diction and grammar. Concisely means that the applicant's presentation should be given succinctly, without digressions. Interviewers are looking for sincerity as well as competence in a candidate. Because body language plays a major role in conveying a candidate's attitude, in an interview situation, applicants need to be aware of how they use facial expressions, eye contact, and gestures to reinforce what they are saying. Applicants also need to listen carefully in order to answer questions directly and establish rapport with the interviewer. Applicants should listen when the interviewer is introduced and use that person's name during the interview. In addition, applicants should listen and allow the interviewer to complete each question before beginning to answer.

Adolescent Literacy and Differentiated Instruction

Teachers can help students prepare for and be more comfortable with interviews by having them assume the parts of applicant and interviewer. Students can practice both job and college admission interviews with their classmates.

Differentiating Interviews

Practice interview sessions afford opportunities to differentiate the content and process. Students can use a local newspaper to find an advertisement for a job they may want to obtain. This can be used as the basis for their interview, with a classmate acting as the employer. Students can also select a college or program they wish to apply to and role-play that interview as well. The process can be differentiated based on how students perform during their first practice interview. The teacher can observe and make notes of each interview. Based on these notes, the teacher can hold individual or small-group minilessons on interview skills. Some helpful interview strategies are listed below.

- Research the company or school holding the interview.
- Anticipate questions that may be asked and plan answers.
- Prepare questions to ask the interviewer.
- Know your strong points and be ready to emphasize them.
- Know your weaknesses and be ready to address them if asked.
- Dress appropriately.
- Speak clearly, correctly, and concisely.
- Maintain good eye contact and posture.
- Be enthusiastic and positive.
- Thank the interviewer.

Informal Speech: Differentiated Instruction, Conversations, and Discussions

Today's English language arts classes are more student-centered than they were in the past. The switch to student-centered learning includes creating opportunities for students to make meaning for themselves. Conversations and small-group discussions support this student-centered learning. Most of the talk that occurs in the classroom is used to make meaning, to support learning. When participating in small- and large-group discussions, students negotiate meaning as they form and test hypotheses. This occurs during discussions when students make observations and raise questions as they listen and respond to others. James Moffett and Betty Jane Wagner (1992) recognize the importance of talk in learning. They suggest that "because constant practice and good interaction are the best teachers of speaking and listening, talk in small groups should be a staple learning activity for all grades and allotted a large amount of time in the curricula" (74). Students socially construct meaning as they participate in group discussions. Robert Probst (2007) notes the importance of collaborative talk: "We need to teach our students to use conversation to build better ideas collaboratively than any of us will come to on our own" (59). Probst also feels that because there are not many good models of civil discourse for our students to learn from, "the schools, in particular English language arts teachers, need to accept that responsibility and make the teaching of discussion a significant part of the curriculum" (45).

Gordon Wells (2003) investigates the relationship between action, talk, reading, writing, and understanding. He has long been a proponent of talk as a necessary component in constructing meaning. Wells finds that there is "a complementary interrelationship between action, talk, and text . . . each of these modes of meaning making is completed and enhanced by the other two" (35). He adds that because making meaning is a social activity, learning depends on collaboration and "such collaboration occurs most naturally and easily through talk about text" (28). For these reasons, he believes that "students' questions and ideas should be welcomed and taken seriously, and opportunities provided for their discussion. Whether in group or whole class settings, such focused discussion is one of the most significant means for students to extend and deepen their understanding as they try to formulate their thoughts in a form appropriate to the emerging exchange of ideas" (1999, 35–36).

In the classroom, this means that students need more opportunities to discuss topics and literature in small-group settings. Being able to talk helps students form opinions and clarify their thoughts. Group discussions, however, do not just happen. Students have to be taught how to participate in peer-led small-group and teacher-led whole-class discussions. True discussions are not recitations. The teacher does not ask a question, call on a student, get an answer, and move on to the next question. In discussions, whether in large or small groups, people talk directly to each other without anyone, including the teacher, orchestrating the talk. This is easier to do successfully in small groups of four to six people; however, whole-class discussions can be successful with practice. Peer-led writing conferences, a special type of group discussions, are explained in Chapter 5. Examples of two popular classroom models for discussion, literature circles and Socratic Seminars, are presented in Chapter 4. These two models share common traits with all forms of successful discussions, which

- have a clear purpose
- take place in a risk-free environment
- encourage participation by all members
- include participants who are prepared to discuss the topic
- include open-ended, meaningful questions

Teachers can provide direct instruction for each of these elements and also model them for the class. In addition, teachers should address the pitfalls of discussions: participants who monopolize the conversation; participants who are unwilling to talk; closed questions with one right answer; questioning or attacking the speaker, not the ideas; and not listening carefully.

It is helpful if the teacher and students together establish a set of ground rules for discussions early in the school year and post them in the classroom. This mutually agreed-upon set of behaviors can be used as a reminder when needed. In addition, at the end of each group discussion, students can evaluate themselves and their group members. Rubrics for group participation can be found online at assessment websites as well as at cooperative learning websites. A more informal assessment can be to use an exit slip after a discussion in which students respond to questions as they leave the classroom, such as: How did I do in our group discussion today? What did I do well? What do I need to improve on? How did our group do as a whole? What can the group do to have better discussions? What help do we need from the teacher?

Group talk is too important a learning tool not to be monitored and supported. The teacher's job during small-group discussions is first to create an atmosphere of trust and respect in the classroom. During small-group discussions, the teacher needs to observe, listen, take notes, and coach when needed. After the discussions, the teacher's job is to elicit self-reflection from the students and to provide feedback based on the observations. Probst (2007) reminds teachers that their role, however, is not just to listen; teachers need to monitor class discussions carefully and to intervene when needed. "The teacher's contribution to the discussion lies in keeping it flowing, making sure that all perspectives are represented and encourage as many kids as possible to enter into the flow of talk, but it's also to enrich and deepen the discourse" (51). There are times when a comment by the teacher may be all a group of students needs to move the discussion forward or to get back on track.

Differentiating Classroom Discussions

In the English language arts class, students can meet to discuss general topics, thematic issues, personal interests, and literary texts. Because students enter the classroom with different degrees of success in discussion groups, the teacher needs to observe participation in group discussions carefully and take notes in order to identify which group's discussion skills need to be reinforced for the whole class and what skills need to be taught to specific students. Small-group instruction can take place during group discussion time. Periodically, the teacher may call the whole class together to reinforce skills and ask how they are doing.

There is some disagreement about how long groups should remain together and what the makeup of the groups should be. A key trait of differentiated instruction is flexible grouping. This means that groups change during the year and even during a unit if appropriate. Groups should not be formed repeatedly based on the same characteristics. For example, if a group membership is based on the same readiness level one time, the teacher should consider grouping students by interests or mixing readiness levels the next time.

Peer groups do not have to be discussing the same thing at the same time. This is a benefit of using small groups and an important component of differentiating. If the purpose of the small-group discussions is to investigate literary devices in a text, for example, groups can be assigned different literary elements to analyze. Groups can also follow different characters throughout a novel or play.

If the purpose of the small-group discussions is to address an issue such as global warming, each group may have a different subtopic to investigate and discuss. After each group has discussed its topic, the groups can share their observations with each other. By mixing groups and offering different topics, the class is richer and more meaningful not just for the students but for the teacher as well.

Differentiated Instruction and Listening

The activities described in the speaking section of this chapter also include listening. Teachers may want to plan lessons that address listening skills directly. In today's digital world, students are bombarded with multimodal communications daily. Many of these involve listening, listening to MP3 players, listening to podcasts, or listening on cell phones. Students also have a selection of material to listen to, including music, novels, speeches, and lectures. Unplugged, students are listening to television shows, dramatic performances, class lectures, peer discussions, and personal conversations. The challenge for teachers is to determine whether their students are really listening or are only hearing the multiple aural texts bombarding them.

Listening is more than hearing. Hearing is a passive activity, whereas listening is an active one. When people listen, they are actively interpreting what they hear, making meaning of it. Listening is similar to reading comprehension. Listeners assess the input they receive aurally against what they already know, assimilating or rejecting the new information. The listener's personal knowledge and background affects the comprehension of new messages. When people listen, they are interpreting the body language of the speaker in addition to what is being said. In addition, different situations call for different types of listening. In social situations, listening can be very demanding because the listener needs to process messages that are received very quickly and may even overlap. In academic situations, students are often called upon to listen and take notes at the same time. And in professional situations, listeners are frequently asked to give an opinion or response to what has just been said.

Because it is so varied, listening is a challenging skill to teach. Like most skills taught in the English language arts classroom, the teacher should introduce effective practices by modeling them for the class. In addition, teachers can give students strategies that will help them become more effective listeners. These strategies include:

- listening with a purpose
- maintaining eye contact
- repeating to yourself what you heard
- maintaining focus on the speaker
- paying attention to visual clues
- waiting for a speaker to finish before making a comment

Teachers can also create activities that allow students to apply these strategies. Academic situations often call for a special type of listening—listening to take notes. Middle and high school students need to learn accurate and efficient ways to listen and take notes. Teachers can share different note-taking strategies and then give students time to practice each one. After being shown different note-taking systems, students usually differentiate the note-taking process on their own by adapting one or more of the strategies to fit their own needs. Three popular note-taking strategies are the Cornell note-taking system, clustering, and informal outlining. In the Cornell note-taking system, students divide the page by drawing a vertical line down the left side, about two inches in from the edge of the paper. To the right of this line, students take notes as they listen to a presentation. The space in the column on the left of the line is for the student to write down observations or questions about the content being recorded on the right-hand side of the page. A system of taking notes based on clustering ideas appeals to many students, especially visual learners. When creating a cluster, the topic or main idea goes into a circle in the middle of the page and subtopics branch off from the center, with facts and examples branching off from them. The subtopics and facts or examples are placed inside bubbles or boxes on the branches. An informal outline is another system that students use when taking notes. In this system, the main topic is listed and subtopics are indented under it. Middle and high school learners can practice using these note-taking systems in classes across the curriculum. Students also need to practice listening in situations that are not academic. Differentiated activities that support active listening are presented in Figure 6–5.

Adolescent Literacy and Differentiated Instruction

Figure 6–5

Listening Tasks Choice Board

Directions for students: Select three tasks to complete from the choice board below.

Find a partner and sit back to back. One of you will speak and one of you will listen and draw. Each of you will hold a geometric pattern out of your partner's sight. Describe the pattern to your partner. Your partner needs to draw what he or she hears you describing. Check the drawing and then switch roles.	Listen to an informative podcast and write a brief summary of what is presented. Then reflect: Were you able to follow the speaker(s)? Was there any part that was difficult to follow? How could the podcast be improved? What differences did you notice between listening to a podcast and listening to a speaker who is in front of you?	Watch a scene from a television show or movie in which two people are communicating. Are they really listening to each other? Identify any strategies they use to listen and suggest how they could listen better. Did you learn any tips about listening from them?
Choose two of the note-taking systems you learned. Take notes in two of your classes, using a different note-taking system for each. Write a reflection on which system you prefer and why.	*Free Choice Square* Students suggest their own tasks. The tasks need to contain some listening element and need to be cleared with the teacher.	Read a scene from a book or short story in which two people are communicating. How does the author convey listening in the story? Suggest other ways to describe listening in a story.
Listen to a story told on the radio, for example on National Public Radio (NPR). What do you notice about your listening behaviors? Write a reflection of how you listened, identifying strategies you used.	Listen to an excerpt from a book on tape or a podcast of a play or book excerpt. Write a reflection on your experience, commenting on how this compares to reading the text.	Watch two people having a conversation and pay attention to their body language and gestures. How do the body language and gestures support or interfere with the communication? Write a summary of what you observe.

Students spend most of their time in English language arts classes speaking and listening, yet these literacies have not received the attention they deserve. Because students enter middle school and high school with a set of speaking and listening skills intact, teachers have focused more on the other literacies of reading, writing, and viewing. A closer look at student proficiency with speaking and listening, however, reveals that the skills students have developed may not be successful ones. Therefore, it is important to include direct instruction and to design practices in speaking and listening so that students can use these skills effectively inside and outside the classroom.

Viewing, Multimedia, and Differentiated Instruction

7

Traditionally English language arts literacies have been divided into reading, writing, speaking, listening, and viewing. "Until recently, language (speech and writing) went largely unchallenged as the communication mode of choice among literate people" (Alvermann 2008, 11). For many years, school curricula around the country reflected this traditional view of communication. Today, however, more English language arts curricula include multimedia and multimodal texts that incorporate visual and audio elements as well as print media. After the National Council of Teachers of English (NCTE) and the International Reading Association (IRA) published their "Standards for the English Language Arts" in 1996, educators began focusing more on multimedia in the classroom. That document recognizes that students need "to read a wide range of print and nonprint texts." The NCTE/IRA standards (1996) also note that students need to "adjust their spoken, written, and visual language to communicate effectively with a variety of audiences for different purposes" (3). Thus, students need to be able to receive and produce information effectively in nonprint formats. Since the publication of the NCTE/IRA standards, an increasing number of states are including the ability to read and understand images in their state standards and on their state tests.

"One aspect of working with multimedia texts is the ability to understand multiple symbol systems. Some educators refer to this as 'intermediality.' Intermediality is defined as 'the ability to critically read and write with and across symbol systems'" (Watts et al. 2000, 208). Students spend a considerable amount time out of school engaging with intermedial texts, such as television, graphic novels, and computer games. Teachers want to help students become more critical readers and viewers of all texts, print and nonprint. Young people's success in today's world depends on being able to view nonprint texts critically and to convey their ideas effectively in nonprint formats.

A second reason for including multimedia texts in the classroom is for motivation. Adolescents learn better when they are motivated and engaged. Multimedia products are high-interest and engaging. Scott Sullivan (2007) finds that "using media as an additional text in the English class is a surefire way to increase the level of involvement for even the most reluctant students" (xv). Unlike those media pioneers of thirty years ago, teachers today have almost limitless resources for teaching media literacy. Teachers who are new to media studies can find helpful resources from the Center for Media Literacy (www.medialit.com) the International Visual Literacy Association (www.ivla.org), and the IRA/NCTE (www.readwritethink.org) websites.

This chapter addresses multiple forms of media, including television, film, and music. It is not a comprehensive study of multimedia sources. It is an overview of media frequently integrated into the English language arts curriculum. Because of the popularity and growth of digital media, they are presented separately in the following chapter on the new literacies.

Visual Literacy and Differentiated Instruction

Media studies frequently begin with an introduction to visual literacy. Before students can critically analyze and respond to a multimedia text, educators recognize that students need to be proficient in viewing—they need to know how to look. For this reason, most state standards include visual literacy as one of their proficiencies. Pailliotet Watts (2000) and her colleagues note that "just as we teach students to be aware of author purpose and text structure in reading, we must also help them identify such organizational structures in viewing and representing ideas through popular and electronic media." To do this, students need to move from passive receivers of visual texts to active viewers. They need to really see what they are looking at.

"Visual literacy is the ability to see, understand, and ultimately to think, create, and communicate graphically" (Thibault and Walbert 2003). Students need to be able to decode what they see and to encode their ideas in visual form. Like the traditional literacy of reading, visual literacy encompasses more than one skill level. As reading print moves from decoding to comprehension, so does visual literacy. The first skill level in visual literacy is identifying the subject or elements of the photograph, work of art, or graphic. Understanding what is seen and comprehending visual relationships is the next level. Truly understanding what is seen requires higher-level critical thinking skills (Thibault and Walbert 2003). Students need to be able to make inferences and analyze visual images in much the same way they do with printed texts.

In 1996, the NCTE adopted a resolution on visual literacy: "Resolved, that the National Council of Teachers of English through its publications, conferences, and affiliates support professional development and promote public awareness of the role that viewing and visually representing our world have as forms of literacy." Michael Day (1997), a member of NCTE's Assembly for Computers in English, added that "although we should attempt to preserve textured notions of literacy, it would be a breach of our duties to ignore the rhetorical powers of visual displays." This resolution sustained the standard on viewing and visual literacy supported by NCTE and IRA (1996): "Being literate . . . means being active, critical, and creative users not only of print and spoken language, but also of the visual language of film and television, commercial and political advertising, photography, and more. Teaching students how to interpret and create visual texts . . . is another essential component of the ELA curriculum" (5).

Students need to be visually literate in order to read and interpret the barrage of images that surround them daily, including charts, photographs, maps, art works, television, movies, Web pages, and social websites. Jim Burke (2001) notes the importance of helping students read visual images: "Through the close reading of these different types of images students reinforce and expand their ability to understand the range of texts they encounter daily" (149). In addition, many books rely on graphics to help communicate their information. Because young people today live in a world that surrounds them with visual messages, most adolescents are quite comfortable with reading and using multimodal texts. The job of the English language arts teacher is to help them do so effectively.

Teachers can begin instruction in visual literacy by using photographs in their lessons. Photographs and other images can be found on the Web; however, teachers should consult with their school librarian or media specialist for information on current copyright laws. Students need to understand that photographs are carefully thought out and edited works, created by the way the photographer selects, focuses, crops, and frames the subject. To practice viewing photographs more critically, students can be taught to ask themselves such questions as What is the subject? From what point of view is the subject photographed? What story does this photo tell? How does lighting affect the photo? How is the subject framed in the photo? What is the setting? What might be just outside this photo? What happened just before this photo was taken? What happened just after this photo was taken? How would this photo be different if the framing or focus were changed slightly? What mood is created in this photo?

These and similar questions can also be applied to works of print art, such as paintings or lithographs. These questions can be introduced by having the teacher model how to apply them to a photograph or work of art. Teachers can also use these questions to create differentiated viewing tasks. Students can be asked to bring to class photographs of their choice and then write analyses using such questions as guides. The students can then share their pictures and analyses with their peers. This is a highly motivational as well as instructional activity. Because the task is differentiated based on interest, each student is connected to the photo he or she selects. Many images can be also obtained on the Internet at sites such as Flickr (www.flickr.com). Another way to introduce visual literacy is to use children's picture books, which are full of wonderful works of art to supplement the narratives. Working in small groups, students can analyze different picture books by focusing on how the artwork is used to enhance or explain the stories. Students can be prompted to look at not only the content but also the form and color used in the art. Figure 7–1 includes tasks that allow students to demonstrate their proficiency with analyzing images in different media.

Figure 7–1

Viewing and Creating Images Tic-Tac-Toe Board

Directions for students: Select three boxes to create tic-tac-toe vertically or diagonally. You may not select three in a row horizontally. Be ready to explain your work to your classmates.

Bring in an image that appeals to you. What medium is it in? Why do you find it interesting or compelling?	Select a poem that we read this year. Bring in an image that you feel supports or helps to interpret the poem.	Bring in an image that puzzles you. What medium is it created in? What do you find puzzling about this image?
Bring in a cartoon that appeals to you. What is the topic of the cartoon? What is its message? Why does it appeal to you?	*Free Choice* Bring in an image of your choice and be ready to explain why you decided to share this image. Clear your choice with the teacher before doing the assignment.	Bring in an image that is related to a book we read this year. What is the medium of the image? How do the image and the text you read work together to convey a message?
Create a cartoon on a topic or theme we studied this year.	Create a visual that conveys a theme of a book we read this year.	Make a photographic collage of a topic or theme we studied this year.

Once students are comfortable with analyzing print images, they can turn to moving images such as those presented on television or in films. Becoming literate with moving images is a necessary part of today's culture. Kevin Kelly (2008), writing for the *New York Times*, explains a paradigm shift he sees happening: "We are now at the middle of a second Gutenberg shift—from book fluency to screen fluency, from literacy to visuality" (48). Although not everyone may agree that society is moving from print to visual literacy, visual literacy is an important part of being literate today.

Film and Differentiated Instruction

Films are used in the English language arts class in three main ways: as a companion to a printed text, as an independent stand-alone text, or as a mode of presentation for student ideas. In the first instance, print and film versions of the same text are often paired, such as a reading of *Romeo and Juliet* paired with a viewing of Zeffirelli's classic film version. In the second instance, films are viewed and analyzed critically in much the same way as printed texts are. The third way film is used in an English language arts classroom is by having students create and film original works that convey their ideas and understanding of a topic being studied.

Most teachers are comfortable and familiar with using film in their English language arts classes to supplement a short story, play, or novel being studied. Teachers either show the film in its entirety after students have read the book, or they show clips from the film while students are the reading the text. Teachers often use films as companion works to printed texts because they find that films can help students better understand literary elements such as setting, plot, theme, and characters. Students often comprehend better what is happening in the book and the themes being addressed if they can see the scenes unfold before them.

When teachers use films or film clips to accompany the reading of a text, there are opportunities to differentiate instruction. Students can be divided into small groups with each group assigned a different literary element to identify, analyze, and then present to the whole class. For this activity, the groups should be academically mixed, as films are accessible to students of all readiness levels. Another way to differentiate is to have each group view a different clip and identify and analyze all of the four elements: setting, plot, theme, and character. If the teacher decides to group students by readiness levels while viewing the film version of a text being studied, a tiered task may be used. Figure 7–2 presents a planning guide and a tiered task for a filmed version of the novel *Hoot* by Carl Hiaasen. Because viewing a film in its entirety takes a considerable amount of class time, some teachers elect to show significant scenes and ask the students to compare the film version to the scene in the book.

Teachers looking for films to teach independent of the literature studied often wonder how to decide what is appropriate for use in the classroom. In addition to checking websites that list films used in schools, teachers could consult "Teaching Visual Literacy: 50 Great Young Adult Films" by Alan B. Teasley and Ann Wilder (1994). Although their annotated list was published in 1994, it contains classics as well as newer titles that are relevant for adolescents, such as *Cinema Paradiso*, *Breaking Away*, and *Gallipoli*. Films can be studied as independent texts to be

Figure 7–2

Planning Guide and Tiered Tasks for Reading and Viewing *Hoot*

Course Title and Level: Grade 8 Language Arts
Unit: Carl Hiaasen's Novel *Hoot*

Essential Questions

How do written versions and film versions of the same book compare?
Why make a movie of a novel?
Why do directors make changes when a novel is made into a film?
How are setting, plot, theme, characters, and symbols portrayed differently in film and in written text?

Unit-Specific Questions

How do the written version and the film version of *Hoot* compare? How are they the same and how do they differ?
What does the film version present that the book cannot?
How does the film help you understand the themes?

Knowledge/Skills

Students will understand the setting, plot, themes, characters, and symbols in Carl Hiaasen's novel *Hoot*.
Students will know how to analyze film and print versions of the same story.

Modes of Differentiation Used

Tiered tasks

Based on (readiness, interests, learning styles)

Readiness

Tier One

Choose a character in the film clip your group is viewing. Make a Venn diagram comparing the character in the scene in the film to the character in the scene in the book. Consider what the character does, what he or she says, and how other characters react to him or her. Your group will hand in a completed Venn diagram.

Tier Two

For the film clip your group is viewing, make a comparison chart for the film and written versions of this scene. The chart should include the setting, plot, characters, and theme.

When thinking about theme, consider what message the author is trying to convey in this scene. You will hand in a written chart for the group.

Tier Three

Filmmakers often use objects as symbols to convey meaning in a scene. In the clip your group is viewing, identify an object that takes on a larger meaning and acts as a symbol for something in the story. Explain how this object works as a symbol to develop character and/or theme. You will hand in a written explanation for your symbol.

viewed and analyzed, or they can be used as bridges to help students understand and analyze printed texts. In either case, students need to begin with a basic viewing vocabulary. John Golden identifies key terms that students of film need to understand, such as *shot, frame, focus, angles, lighting, sound,* and *editing.* In his book *Reading in the Dark: Using Film as a Tool in the English Classroom* (2001), Golden presents detailed explanations of each term, plus suggested films for teaching them.

When teaching films as independent texts, teachers emphasize looking at each element and analyzing how it affects a scene. For example, students may be asked to look closely at a scene with the sound turned off in order to concentrate on the angles of the shots and the lighting. Students are taught to do a close reading of a film in much the same way they do a close reading of a literary text. Teachers and students today have film resources on DVDs that can help with this. Many movies now available on DVD contain extra information on the production of the film, including commentaries on the cinematic devices used. In addition to learning how to view a film by focusing on the terms listed in the viewing vocabulary mentioned earlier, teachers can create film studies based on different film genres, such as mystery, detective, action/adventure, drama, horror, romance, musical, and comedy. Studying the different film genres presents another opportunity to differentiate instruction by allowing students to choose a genre they would like to study more closely. Students may work alone or in small groups to review the genre and then view and analyze a film in that genre.

Although Golden (2001) sees the benefits of teaching films as independent texts in their own right, he is also a proponent of using films as a bridge to reading literature. He observes that many of the same strategies used when viewing are also used when reading: predicting, responding to text, questioning, and visualizing (59). Golden also finds that teaching students how to use these skills when viewing films improves their ability to do so when reading literature. He also found that more advanced literary analysis skills such as identifying and analyzing irony or symbols can also be introduced visually. For example, to present a symbol, a director may have the camera focus on an object and then show that object later in the same form or altered in some way, thus highlighting it as a symbol. One of the most famous symbols in film is the sled "Rosebud" in Orson Welles' *Citizen Kane.* Symbols can appear in both the printed text and in the film version of a story. For example, in *Lord of the Flies*, Piggy's glasses and the conch shell appear in both works. Irony can also be explained more clearly for some students by presenting a visual example because, as Golden notes, "The meaning intended by the director (or writer) is the exact opposite of what he or she appears to be presenting" (89). In a film, irony may be seen by presenting visually incongruous images or by providing seemingly incongruous music on a soundtrack. When, for example, scenes of battle and death are shown in *Good Morning Vietnam*, the soundtrack is the song "What a Wonderful World" (89). To differentiate literary devices presented in visual format, teachers could have students find their own examples of literary elements such as irony or symbolism in films they select and explain these to the class.

Students can create their own films as a way to convey their understanding of a theme or their interpretation of a print text. Making films has become easier; as Kevin Kelly (2008) observes, "Because of new consumer gadgets, community training, peer encouragement and fiendishly clever software, the ease of making video now approaches the ease of writing" (48). Asking students to create their own films is a good way to differentiate products, especially for visual learners. A popular strategy for students to demonstrate their understanding of a text they have read is to ask them to create a book trailer. A book trailer is like a movie trailer in that it includes visual images, printed text, and a soundtrack. A movie trailer is used to introduce a movie and to persuade the public to go see it. The trailer's job is to "sell" the movie. Book trailers can do the same thing for novels or plays the students have read. Before students film this or any other project, they need to know how to plan a film ahead of time by creating a storyboard. Storyboards graphically represent what is to be seen in each shot of the film. For the book trailer project, students can work alone, with a partner, or in a small group to create a two- to three-minute trailer for a book they read. For example, in a class using literature circles, each group can create a book trailer to present to those who have not read their book. To produce the book trailers, students can use the technology of digital movie cameras and iMovies or simple video cameras alone. Figure 7–3 is a differentiated planning guide for this activity. Another version of this activity is described by Scott Williams (2007), who had his students work in small groups and required that the groups include reasons for the scenes they created in their storyboards for the book trailers. Williams found that

Figure 7–3

Planning Guide and Assignment for Book Trailer

Course Title and Level: Sophomores: Classic American Novels
Unit: Literature Circles on the Theme "Coming of Age"

Essential Questions

How are coming-of-age stories similar across cultures and time?
What does a coming-of-age story reveal about life?
Why do coming-of-age stories endure?
Why do coming-of-age stories appeal to today's adolescents?
How is coming of age both a physical and a mental journey?

Unit-Specific Questions

How can a video be used to convince someone to read?
What are the key aspects to include when "selling" a book?

Knowledge/Skills

Students will create a collaborative product.
Students will create storyboards for planning.
Students will know the key points of book read by the group.
Students will produce a book trailer.

Modes of Differentiation Used

Differentiate content of reading material
Differentiate products

Based on (readiness, interests, learning styles)

Interests for book selection
Readiness for technology

Different Book Trailers

Assignment: Working in small groups, students create two- to three-minute book trailers for texts their groups have read. First, they need to complete a storyboard to be approved by the teacher before filming. Students can use technology such as digital video cameras and the iMovie computer application. If this technology is not available, students can use video cameras.

Texts include:

The Adventures of Huckleberry Finn by Mark Twain

The Red Badge of Courage by Stephen Crane

My Antonia by Willa Cather

The Catcher in the Rye by J. D. Salinger

Their Eyes Were Watching God by Zora Neale Hurston

"because they are so invested in this project, the students give one another ample support in crafting their written analyzes, and overall, these are the best written products I receive all year" (107).

Students can also create a film text by working in groups to create a scene that did not happen in a novel but might have. This activity can be differentiated by having each group decide where their scene would fit into the novel. One group of students, for example, created a scene for *The Scarlet Letter* in which Arthur Dimmesdale returns to the scaffold in the daylight and confesses his sin. Students should create storyboards for their scenes, film the scenes, and then share the films with the whole class. Figure 7–4 includes a planning guide and assignment for differentiating this activity. A variation on this activity is to have the groups write a sequel—what happens after the story ends. Many of the elements of viewing that students apply to films also apply to watching television.

Television and Differentiated Instruction

Television images, unlike printed words, come already decoded for the viewer. The viewer literally sees what is happening. But like reading, viewing comprehension is more than decoding. To comprehend the images, the viewer needs to carry on an "internal dialogue with the creators of a program" ("What Is Critical Viewing?" 2008, 1). Viewers need to watch actively, challenge, analyze, and react to the medium. When watching television dramas and comedies, students can be taught to pay attention to the plot as well as to the soundtrack and the filming techniques. Students can be shown that the plot in most television comedies and dramas follows the same story arc as in a short story: exposition, rising action, climax, falling action, and conclusion. Students can watch a comedy and a drama and write down a plot outline for each show. This activity can be easily differentiated by allowing the students to self-select the shows or by having them select shows from a teacher-prepared list. For some students, identifying the plot development in a show they watch can help them better understand how the plot develops in a story or novel. As with any new assignment, teachers should introduce or review the key concepts and model an example with the whole class.

To help students understand how different elements of television work, teachers can have students turn the sound off when they are watching a show.

Figure 7–4

Planning Guide: Creating and Filming a Scene

Course Title and Level: Grade 11 English

Unit: Novel Study

Essential Questions

How does the addition of a scene in a novel affect the story?

How can stories be represented in different modes?

How are scenes for films created?

Unit Specific Questions

How would the narrative change if a new scene were added to the story?

How can this scene be portrayed in film?

What is the role of storyboards in filming?

Knowledge/Skills

Students will know how to create a new scene to insert into an existing work of literature.

Students will understand how each scene is related to a novel as a whole.

Students will know how to create a storyboard to plan for filming a scene.

Students will know how to film a scene based on a storyboard.

Students will be able to present and explain their work to the whole class.

Modes of Differentiation Used

Product: differentiate by choice

Based on (readiness, interests, learning styles)

Product: based on interests

Assignment:

Working in small groups, students decide on a scene that did not happen in the novel but might have. Group members create the scene and present it in storyboard format. After completing the storyboard, they film the scene for viewing by the whole class.

Variation:

Working in groups, students extend the ending of the novel by adding a scene that could happen next. Group members create the scene and present it in storyboard format. After completing the storyboard, they film the scene for viewing by the whole class.

When watching a comedy, this has an immediate impact. Without hearing the "canned laughter," students need to ask themselves, "Does it seem as funny?" The same strategy can be used when watching a drama, for example, a crime show. Students should ask themselves, "What is the effect of watching without the background sound effects and music?" This can be a good activity to do as a whole class. It is not necessary to watch a whole program. Clips from television shows can be used.

The filming techniques of television can also be studied. There are some TV programs today using more nontraditional filming techniques, for example, filming scenes with handheld cameras. The students can compare this to traditional filming techniques and discuss the differences between the two. They can also look at the lighting on shows and ask: "Why are some shows so dark? Why are other shows lit in almost a cartoonlike fashion? What is the impact of lighting on the viewer?"

Students need to realize that they are being manipulated when they watch television. The network program directors and producers decide what programs are put on television and at what times those shows are aired. Advertisers generally decide which commercials to pair with any particular show. Television commercials afford the teacher an opportunity to introduce propaganda techniques in advertising. Scott Sullivan (2007), coeditor of *Lesson Plans for Creating Media-Rich Classrooms*, observes that by "making students aware of the ways information is used and manipulated, we allow them to begin making wiser, more informed choices" (176). Students need to be informed consumers of advertisements and commercials. Persuasive devices used in advertising, propaganda techniques actually, can be introduced by having students look closely at print ads from magazines and newspapers before asking them to analyze television commercials. Teachers can also present digitalized copies of ads for the whole class to analyze, many of which can be accessed online at Duke University's Ad*Access site at http://guides.library.duke.edu/image. After introducing basic persuasive devices, students are asked to identify the devices in print ads. Figure 7–5 presents a list of basic persuasive devices and a differentiated tiered task for identifying them in print ads. Once students are familiar with identifying and analyzing persuasion in print advertisements, they can apply the same strategies to viewing television commercials.

Figure 7–5

Common Persuasive Devices and Tiered Differentiated Assignment

The following persuasive devices can be found in print and multimedia advertisements.

Bandwagon: everyone is doing it, therefore you should.

Card stacking: telling only one side of an argument, includes slanted language.

Emotional appeal: appeals to strong negative or positive feelings we have.

Flag waving: it is the patriotic thing to do.

Glittering generalities: general, glowing terms are used to say how great a product is without substantial proof.

Name calling: using negative or derogatory words, especially about a person.

Plain folks: people just like you and me agree.

Snob appeal: only the best is good enough, or only the best people use this.

Testimonial: an expert or famous person says so.

Transfer: showing famous people near a product without quoting them directly.

Tiered Differentiated Assignment

Tier One

Look through magazines and newspapers to find advertisements that represent each of the persuasive devices listed above. Identify which device is represented in each ad you find.

Tier Two

Look through magazines and newspapers to find an example of each of the persuasive devices listed above. Identify the audience for each ad you find. Next explain which ad you feel is most effective and why.

Tier Three

Look through magazines and newspapers to find an example of each of the persuasive devices listed above. Identify who you believe the intended audience is for each ad you find. Next, choose an ad to analyze, explaining how the visual layout of the ad and the printed text work together to convey a message to the intended audience.

Mark Ziminski, a teacher at South Brunswick High School in New Jersey, teaches his eleventh-grade students an advertising unit each year at Super Bowl time. Mark begins the unit teaching rhetorical and persuasive devices. In addition to persuasive devices such as those listed in Figure 7–5, Mark reviews the classical rhetorical devices of logos, pathos, ethos, and logical fallacies. The students watch a number of commercials from Super Bowl history and complete an analysis of a few of these commercials as a whole class. The students then get to select one of the ads to write about for their final analyses. The students are able to view each ad three times, taking notes as they watch during class time. In addition to identifying the persuasive and rhetorical devices in the commercials, the students analyze the commercials for targeted audience, image appeal, slogans, and motive. Motive is divided into four types: protection, relief, acquisition, and prevention.

Students can be more discriminating viewers if they are familiar with the range of television offerings and the commercials associated with them. Figure 7–6 is a menu board for watching and analyzing television shows and commercials. After the students have completed their tasks, they meet in groups and compare the findings. The whole class then discusses the conclusions each group has reached. Another example of a differentiated assignment for viewing commercials is presented in Figure 7–7, which contains a planning guide as well as a differentiated task. The television assignments help students understand that they are being manipulated by the content of both the programs and the commercials, thus becoming more discriminating viewers. Students also need to be aware that every time they watch a show they are making choices. We can help them make more informed choices.

Visual and Auditory Literacy and Differentiated Instruction

Matthew Cinotti, an English teacher at West Morris Central High School (New Jersey), also teaches a course in media literacy. This course encompasses learning about and becoming literate in a variety of visual and auditory media, including film, television, and music. Matthew has devised and delivered a two-week unit on music that is differentiated according to students' interests and readiness. Each day, at the start of the period, the teacher begins with a ten-minute

Figure 7–6

Television Analysis Choice Board

Directions for students: Select one task from each row.

Watch a television program that is on between 7 P.M. and 8 P.M. Then watch a show that is on between 9 P.M. and 11 P.M. Compare the two shows based on intended audience, content, and format. What conclusions can you draw?	Watch a television show that is on between 9 P.M. and 11 P.M. on a major network channel. Then watch a show that is on the same time and on a cable channel. Compare the two shows based on intended audience, content, and format. What conclusions can you draw?	Watch a television show that is on a major network on Saturday morning between 8 A.M. and 11 A.M. and compare it to a show that is on a Public Broadcasting channel (PBS) at the same time. Compare the two shows based on intended audience, content, and format. What conclusions can you draw?
Watch a television show that is on between 8 P.M. and 9 P.M. and pay attention to the commercials, noting the products and the intended audiences. What persuasive devices did you notice? What conclusions can you draw?	Watch a television show that is on between 9 P.M. and 11 P.M. and pay attention to the commercials, noting the products and the intended audiences. What persuasive devices did you notice? What conclusions can you draw?	Watch a television show that is on Saturday morning between 8 A.M. and 11 A.M. and pay attention to the commercials, noting the products and the intended audiences. What persuasive devices did you notice? What conclusions can you draw?
Watch a television news program on a major network and watch one on a cable network. Compare the two, noting the type of information given, amount of opinions included, and the demeanor of the reporter. What conclusions can you draw?	Watch a television program on nature. What channel is it on? What time of day is it shown? Who is the intended audience? What types of commercials are shown? What is playing on a network channel at the same time? What conclusions can you draw?	Watch a home improvement program. What channel is it on? What time of day is it shown? Who is the intended audience? What types of commercials are shown? What show is on a network channel at the same time? What conclusions can you draw?

Figure 7–7

Viewing Commercials Planning Guide and Assignment

Course Title and Level: Grade 9 English
Unit: Persuasion in Media

Essential Questions

Why do we make the purchases we do?
How can a viewer be persuaded to buy a product?
How do advertisements change based on the audience?

Unit-Specific Questions

How are persuasive devices integrated into the advertisements we see in print and on television?
Why is it important for adolescents to be familiar with advertising techniques?

Knowledge/Skills

Students will know basic persuasive devices advertisers use.
Students will know how ads are constructed.
Students will know how to analyze the visuals and the written texts in advertisements.
Students will know how to read or view advertisements critically.

Modes of Differentiation Used

Content: differentiate content in the form of the commercials chosen

Based on (readiness, interests, learning styles)

Interests

Assignment

Part One

Students will choose two different time slots to watch television commercials on the same day.
These times need to be at least two hours apart. Students will watch all the commercials for a
complete thirty- or sixty-minute program. Students will keep a record of the type and length
of the program, the number of commercials during the program, and the products of the
commercials. Students will then make an inference about the audience for the commercials.
Students will also make note of any persuasive devices they recognize in the commercials.

Part Two

Working in small groups, students will compare their findings from the shows they watched
and the commercials they analyzed. Looking at their results, each group will report its
observations on how advertisers use television shows to sell products.

introduction to some aspect of popular music: innovation in music recording; 1900–1950; early rock and roll, doo wop; Motown; jazz; folk and folk rock; glam rock; punk rock; 1970s; grunge; alternative; R&B; rap; hip-hop. Students then have the remainder of the period to work on their choice board activities or their independent research projects (see Figure 7–8). They can choose to research, analyze, or create. Multiple ways of demonstrating what they have learned include completing a graphic organizer, incorporating digital pictures, and writing a formal commentary. The responses students offer are further differentiated by the teacher, who offers students the opportunity to choose how they are to be evaluated, as long as their total projects all add up to same amount, in this case, eight points. The rubric, included in Figure 7–8, judges the finished products on the same criteria of professionalism, effort, creativity, and accuracy.

Students encounter multimedia texts daily, at school and at home. Viewing and listening to texts are as important in the adolescent world as reading the printed word. Teachers need to integrate different text forms into the curriculum so that their students can respond critically to the variety of texts available to them today and tomorrow.

Figure 7–8

Music Unit Choice Board and Rubric

Directions for students: For this unit, you can choose how you would like to be evaluated. From the chart below, you can select any of the choices, but you must total at least eight points.

Research	Analysis	Creation
Diagram (two points): Select a genre of music and research the background information of that genre. Create a graphic organizer for that genre showing the following: a definition, a brief history (what genres does it come from), what character-istics all music in this genre share, examples of songs, nonexamples, and your own visual representation of the genre.	Evaluate (three points): Using your favorite songs and your least favorite songs, in a write-up search for trends among these songs to explain why you like the songs you do.	Draw (four points): Pick a song of your choosing and create a symbolic picture for the song (one moment of the song or the entire movement of the piece). Create a one-page write-up explaining your picture.
Compare (three points): Find a song that has been remade and research both the original song and the remake. Find out information about the artists and the time period of each song. In a Venn diagram or another suitable chart, compare and contrast the two pieces, using the background information you found to explain the juxtaposition.	Analyze lyrics (four points): Analyze the lyrics in a song of your choosing, paying attention to rhetorical devices to explain how they contribute to the overall theme, mood, or tone of the piece. This would take the form of a commentary.	Perform (five points): Write a song with original music and lyrics. Perform it for the class and provide an explanation of your song, paying attention to how the music and lyrics complement each other.

continued on next page

Figure 7–8 *continued from previous page*

Research	Analysis	Creation
Discuss (three points): Select two artists from different genres and research information about them. Select a song from a third genre, and create a transcript of a hypothetical critique the two artists might have made of this song. This can take the form of a script of a movie review show.	Analyze visual (four points): Produce a visual analysis of a music video, album cover, or a commercial that uses a famous song by decoding, interpreting, and critically analyzing the piece to explain how the visual goes along with the music and lyrics.	Construct (six points): Using a song or poem of your choosing, take digital pictures (of your own or from the Internet) that fit with the audio you've chosen to create a digital story or music video.

Music Unit Rubric

Name: _____

Activity: _____

	Professionalism	Effort	Creativity	Accuracy
9–10	• Is easy to follow • Shows evidence of editing • Is easy to read • Is a finished product	• Shows evidence of strong effort • Shows a high level of work went into the project • Is up to the student's usual ability level (based on past projects)	• Is very creative, original • Addresses assignment in an entertaining, informative, and unique way	• All material and content are accurate • Information is logical • No claims are unsubstantiated

continued on next page

Figure 7–8 *continued from previous page*

	Professionalism	Effort	Creativity	Accuracy
7–8	• Could be clearer to follow logic of piece • Has grammatical mistakes or rough ends but some evidence of editing • For the most part is a finished product	• Shows evidence of effort • Shows the student put work into project • May not necessarily be up to the student's usual caliber of work	• Is creative • May not be wholly original • Is at least entertaining, informative, or unique	• All major content is accurate, with only minor inaccuracies • Information may need to be clearer in logic to back up all claims
5–6	• Is not really a finished product • Could have clearer logic • Has many rough ends about it	• Shows little evidence of effort • Shows that the student put a minimal amount of effort into the project • Is nowhere near the student's usual caliber of work	• Has minor evidence of creativity • Is not really original but rather a rehashing of another's ideas • May be entertaining or informative	• Major inaccuracies or unsubstantiated claims in the presentation of material

_____ /40 × _____ = _____
Total points   Point value   Total weighted
above   for task   points for this task

_____ /8 × 100 = _____
Points from   Total grade
each task

The New Literacies and Differentiated Instruction

8

Since the late 1990s, the term *new literacies* has been appearing with more frequency in professional journals, research reports, and school curricula. Today, young people rely heavily on electronic resources for the reading and writing they are doing outside the classroom; in fact, their use of electronic resources is becoming greater than their use of pen and paper. As many teachers realize, "Digital literacies are here to stay. They are the core of the new literacies" (O'Brien and Barber 2008, 68).

Changes in technology and text forms have forced educators to rethink the definition of literacy. But, as Donald Leu (2004) and his colleagues found, "We lack a precise definition of what the new literacies are"; they do, however, agree that the new literacies "include skills and strategies necessary for successful use and adaptation to the rapidly changing information and communication technologies" and that educators' view of literacy must change to "include electronic environments" (1583–84). Susan Armstrong and David Warlick (2005) echo this thought: "We need to redefine literacy in an increasingly digitalized and networked world" (1). In 2001, The International Reading Association published *Integrating Literacy and Technology into the Curriculum: A Position Statement*, which addresses the new literacies, noting: "The Internet and other forms of information and communication technology (ICT) such as word processors, Web editors, presentation software, and e-mail are regularly redefining the nature of literacy. To become fully literate in today's world, students must become proficient in the new literacies of ICT." Since the publication of that document, the technological resources available to students have continued to expand. In order for adolescents to work successfully with these new technologies, they need new literacy skills that many are calling the 4E's to supplement the traditional 3R's. Students need the ability to: expose knowledge, explain information, express ideas, and practice ethics on the Internet (Armstrong and Warlick 2005).

Kathleen Yancey (2008), writing in the National Council of Teachers of English (NCTE) *Council Chronicle*, reports on the findings of an NCTE committee investigating what readers and writers in the twenty-first century need: to develop proficiency with technology and to create, critique, analyze, and evaluate multimedia texts (68). Students today are engaging in multimodal discourse, and as teachers we need to prepare them to be able to read and contribute to this discourse in meaningful ways.

Because the way adolescents receive and construct meaning is changing, researchers are taking a new look at their reading and writing practices. Current research finds that reading and writing online is not the same as off-line. New technologies "have the potential to make writing more fluid and facilitate the blending of visual and verbal texts" (NCTE 2008b, 16). Writing online gives students new purposes, contexts, and audiences for their work. Concerning changes in reading, the New Literacies Research Team at the University of Connecticut has found that online reading comprehension is not identical to off-line reading comprehension. They found that the questions readers ask themselves differ. They also found that reading and writing are more integrated when using the new technologies. In addition, they caution that students need to be more critical readers of the texts they access online (Leu 2008). Julie Coiro's (2003) findings support this view of reading online: "Web-based texts are typically nonlinear, interactive, and inclusive of multiple media forms" (459). It is clear that reading and writing can no longer be seen as print-only media.

The Internet has opened a new world of opportunities for adolescent readers and writers, changing the way young people access, retrieve, and use information. Student use of the Internet has led The New Literacies Research Team to conclude that "the Internet is this generation's defining technology for literacy and learning" (Coiro et al. 2008). Students' use of the Internet is so extensive that young people today are often referred to as the Web 2.0 generation. A recent report from the James R. Squire Office of Policy Research states, "Reading and writing are being transformed textually, relationally, spatially, and temporally" (NCTE 2008a, 16). Textually, text formats are changing to include multimedia representations along with the printed word. Relationally, the new media increases social interaction and reflective conversation. Spatially, reading and writing are being conducted at new literary sites, such as 'zines, fan fiction, and performance poetry websites. Temporally, the time boundaries are being collapsed by practices such as instant messaging and distance learning (NCTE 2008a, 18).

The Internet is at the core of many of the new instructional strategies used by English language arts teachers. The hypertext environment of the Internet that allows students to move in different directions helps teachers tailor assignments based on student readiness, interests, and learning styles. Assignments can be differentiated by giving students the freedom to pursue different Internet links while exploring a common topic. The Internet is one of many tools classroom teachers use to differentiate instruction.

The new digital technologies appeal to adolescents in part because of the sense of community found in online discourse communities. Students can communicate instantly with a real audience and receive feedback on their ideas as well as on the texts they are composing. In addition, many students enjoy using technology to create multimodal texts that incorporate visuals, including videos, into their written work. Multimodal texts have a special appeal for students whose learning preferences are more visual. Because of the visual supports they offer, multimodal texts are more accessible for many struggling readers and nonnative speakers of English than traditional printed texts.

Not only is our definition of literacy changing but the new literacies themselves are evolving. This rapid change makes writing about the new literacies a challenge. What is new today may be old tomorrow. Teachers, however, cannot wait to see what will develop tomorrow. Young people are using new media today, and we need to look at how this use can be incorporated effectively into the classroom.

This chapter is not a comprehensive discussion of technology in the classroom; rather, it offers an overview of technological and multimodal resources and classroom practices that can support differentiated instruction. As noted earlier, the risk with providing a list of new media is the rate at which they change. The following list contains some of the technological practices currently being used in middle and secondary classrooms to support literacy learning:

- word processing
- writing online
- digital portfolios
- Internet searches
- electronic texts (e-texts)
- WebQuests
- electronic bulletin boards
- blogs
- vlogs (video blogs)
- wikis
- podcasts
- Web pages
- PowerPoint presentations
- video presentations
- digital storytelling
- graphic novels
- mangas
- virtual classrooms
- distance learning

Because the focus of this book is on popular classroom applications of the new literacies, we have not included social networking sites or text messaging.

Although some teachers are beginning to integrate social networking sites into lessons such as memoir writing, many schools block access to such sites because of the unmonitored content they contain.

The digital tools available today can be intriguing and fun; however, when teachers think about incorporating new technology into the curriculum, they need to do so with a clear purpose in mind. Sara Kajder (2006) reminds teachers that technology should not be used just because it is available. Teachers need to keep in mind the goals of the lesson or unit. They need to ask themselves: How do these tools support the learning goals for this lesson or unit? What can these tools help the students do that cannot be done in a more traditional way? What are the benefits of using these multimodal or digital tools? Will these tools help all students or should they be an option only for some? How can I use these tools to differentiate my lessons when needed? Teachers need to keep the learning goals in mind and remember that the new technologies and differentiated instruction are not ends in themselves but classroom practices employed to help all students learn better. In addition, it is not a question of using information and communication technology or pen and paper for instruction, but integrating them all into our lessons to help every student to be a successful learner. Technology and multimodal texts should be integrated into the English language arts classroom because they

- motivate adolescent learners
- foster collaboration
- offer authentic reasons for reading and writing
- help adolescents develop voice
- provide feedback from peers and adults
- address multiple learning styles
- integrate reading, writing, speaking, and listening
- make learning personal and confidential
- promote analytical and critical thinking

Digital technologies and multimodal texts provide teachers with new tools that can be used for differentiating instruction to meet the needs of students who learn in multiple ways. The application section that follows focuses on selected digital technologies that support differentiating instruction in the classroom. When creating assignments integrating new media, teachers need to be aware that students are at different levels of comfort and expertise when it comes to using technology. However, as Kajder reminds us, "The right tool when paired with the right task and the right student can yield tremendous results" (2006, 36).

Podcasts and Differentiated Instruction

Podcasts are play-on-demand digital audio or visual files that can be distributed over the Internet. They can be accessed by a personal computer or downloaded to a portable MP3 player. They can also be burned onto a CD. Like other new literacies media, they integrate reading, writing, speaking, and listening. Students can listen to or view professionally produced podcasts or they can make their own. Because podcasts are relatively simple to produce and are quite engaging, they offer an attractive medium for classroom use.

Podcasts can be created by teachers or by students in three basic stages: preproduction, production, and postproduction. Preproduction includes planning, scripting, revising, rehearsing, and choosing sound effects. Production entails setting up materials and recording the podcast in short segments. In order to record, a person requires a microphone and software that records sound such as Audacity or GarageBand. Both are free downloads from the Internet. Postproduction includes editing and publishing the podcast online (Hess 2008). To publish online, the class needs an Internet website such as a wiki. A blogging component (writing in response to the content of a website) can be added by having students respond at the same online site after listening to the podcast. Podcasts can also be saved to CDs and then played on student computers in class or at home. There are many websites for teachers who want to learn more about podcasting or need help producing them, including www.podcasting-tools.com and www.podomatic.com.

One way to incorporate podcasts into an English language arts classroom is to connect them to the literature being read. Adolescents can be reluctant readers, especially when asked to read more challenging texts such as the classics. Rebekah Hess (2008) sees podcasts as a way into literature study. "In order to open up these texts to their students, teachers must explore new ways of presenting the material. Podcasting is an excellent medium for engaging students" (1). Because podcasts are usually on the Web, they can be accessed both inside and outside the classroom. This extends the classroom community beyond the physical classroom space. In addition, podcasts have the potential to provide a worldwide audience, making them an authentic learning experience. Students are motivated learners when they know their ideas are being heard. Will Richardson (2006), a proponent of technology in the classroom, sees an important benefit of using the new technology. "Our students are learning that their voices matter, that people are listening and responding, that their ideas count" (129).

Podcasts are a versatile tool in the classroom. They fit into almost any unit of study, including presenting new vocabulary words, book reports, literary discussions, dramatic performances, and project presentations. A traditional assignment in English language arts classrooms is to have students read a text independently and then report on it to the whole class. Using a podcast, each student can orally present a review of a book and class members can give feedback on it in writing. Teachers can also create whole units of study based on podcasting—for example, having the class create a series of radio shows or present a reader's theatre.

Sara Kajder (2004) reports on another way she used podcasts in the classroom. Her class was writing essays on bullying and what students believed was the real reason behind bullying. In order to make this assignment more interactive, Kajder gave her students the option to record their essays on Audacity for posting on her class electronic bulletin board, or eBoard, so that their parents and classmates could hear them. Kajder suggests another way to have students complete this assignment: post the essays on a website such as www.thisibelieve.com.

Hess (2008) cautions that there can be some problems when using podcasts, and teachers need to plan ahead carefully to avoid these. Teachers should obtain permission slips from parents before posting podcasts publicly on the Internet. In addition, to avoid copyright issues, teachers should remind students that all work posted needs to be original. Rubrics should be presented at the beginning of a podcast project to make it clear to the students what work is expected and how it will be assessed. A number of podcast rubrics are readily available on the Internet. Teachers can locate these by typing "podcast rubrics" into their Internet search engines. Typical categories on a podcast rubric include: introduction, format/organization, information, artwork, audio/music, and group/partner work. Finally, teachers need to make certain that the podcast connects to the unit goals. It is easy to get caught up in the fun aspect of this technology, but never lose sight of the reasons for using it—to help students become creative and critical thinkers and to help students learn the content better.

As with other media of the new literacies, podcasts present multiple opportunities for differentiating instruction. Teachers who use podcasts in their classes can differentiate the content, the process, and the product for their assignments. The content can be varied based on the interests of the students. If the class is creating a radio show about their school as a podcast, students can choose different areas of interest to report on during the podcast, such as sports, academics, people in the news, and upcoming events. During the production stage, students can take on different roles based on their interests and readiness levels. Students who prefer to write or who show strengths in this area can work on scripting the show. Students who prefer more visual tasks can be involved in the video production. And students who have demonstrated good organizational skills can work on coordinating the whole production process. In the postproduction stage, technologically savvy students can make certain the podcast is uploaded to the class wiki or another selected website. All of these tasks can be designed to be individual or collaborative projects. After a podcast has been uploaded onto a website, students can view and listen to the contents and then write their reactions to it on the website as they would on any blog. The teacher can direct the responses of the students by posing specific questions for them to address, for example, questions that ask students to reflect on their own learning during the process or questions that ask them to evaluate the effectiveness of the presentation.

Teachers can also differentiate literature studies using podcasts. After reading *Hamlet*, students can be divided into groups to analyze different literary devices in the play, with each group preparing a section of a class podcast on the play. Teachers can differentiate the content by assigning specific literary devices to each group based on the readiness of each student. At the end of the podcast, each group might post questions or quotations for their classmates to think about and respond to on the class website. When the work is posted online or burned onto a CD, students are able to listen to their classmates' analyses and respond to them on their own time, either in class or at home. Allowing students to work at their own speed is another way to differentiate the process for each student. Figure 8–1 offers a planning guide for differentiating podcasts for a unit on *Hamlet*, and Figure 8–2 contains the tiered

Figure 8–1

Planning Guide for *Hamlet* Podcast

Course Title and Level: Grade 12 English

Unit: *Hamlet*

Essential Questions

How does an author use imagery to develop character and theme?

How does an author use motif to develop theme?

How can creating and viewing a podcast help students understand imagery and motif?

Unit-Specific Questions

How does Shakespeare use imagery of disease, nature, and poison in *Hamlet* to develop character and theme?

How does a spying motif develop character and theme in *Hamlet*?

How can creating and responding to a podcast help students understand character and theme in *Hamlet*?

Knowledge/Skills

Students will understand imagery: disease, nature, poison.

Students will understand the spying motif.

Students will know how to produce a podcast.

Modes of Differentiation Used

Students will present a literary analysis orally.

Content: Differentiate topic by teacher-assigned groups based on readiness levels.

Process: Differentiate roles in producing a podcast based on student interests.

Strategy: tiered tasks

Figure 8–2

Tiered Podcasts for Imagery and Motif in *Hamlet*

For each podcast, group members decide who will take on the different roles in creating the podcast: scripting, producing, revising, and posting. Each group needs to turn in a written plan for creating the podcast before beginning production.

Tier One

Working as a group, create a podcast that identifies two examples of poison imagery in the play and explain how this imagery helps to develop themes in the play. At the end of your podcast, present questions or quotations for your classmates to think about and respond to.

Tier Two

Working as a group, create a podcast that identifies at least three examples of nature imagery in the play and explain how these examples develop both character and theme in the play. At the end of your podcast, present questions or quotations for your classmates to think about and respond to.

Tier Three

Working as a group, create a podcast that identifies at least three examples of disease imagery in the play and explain how these examples support both character development and theme in the play. At the end of your podcast, present questions or quotations for your classmates to think about and respond to.

Tier Four

Working as a group, create a podcast that explains how spying acts as a motif in the play to develop character and theme. At the end of your podcast, present questions or quotations for your classmates to think about and respond to.

assignment based on that plan. The rationale for using podcasts in this assignment is twofold: first, students need practice with public speaking, and second, students are more motivated and more likely to do their best work when they know a real audience is going to be listening to and learning from what they say.

Blogs and Differentiated Instruction

For many years, a secondary English teacher had a bulletin board in the front of her English classroom with the message "Think About It" at the top. Under this heading was a quotation or saying that would change periodically. Students from each of the five daily class periods were invited to think and respond to the message by writing directly on the blank paper beneath the quotation. The point was not only to have students think about a meaningful saying, but also to have them communicate with students from other class periods who would respond to both the quotation and the comments their peers made. Blogging is the twenty-first century version of the "Think About It" board. It can serve the same purpose—to create a discourse community by providing a place for students to voice their opinions and raise questions for a real audience. Kajder (2007) believes that "real writing" for kids happens not in classroom assignments but in blogs and other electronic sites (214). It can be a challenge for English language arts teachers to make classroom assignments as close to "real writing" as possible. Blogging helps do this.

Blog is the common name for a Web log, an electronic bulletin board or journal on the Internet. Blogs first began appearing in 1997 and have grown steadily since the advent of do-it-yourself online blogging tools in 1999 (Williams and Jacobs 2004). Also in 1999, *edublog* began appearing as a term for blogging for instructional purposes. In this chapter, we use the overarching term *blog* to refer to both educational and noneducational blogs. Blogs combine the traditional literacies of reading and writing with the technological advantages of word processing and Internet links. Visitors to a blog read the entries and respond to the content directly on the site. The entries are dated and appear sequentially, much like a diary. The content of a blog may be exclusively verbal or it may contain images and hypertext links to other websites. Some blogs also contain an audio component. Blogs have a great appeal to adolescents. Henning (2003) found that 51.5 percent of the blogs were written by authors between the ages of 13 and 19. Many of our students are already blogging; they are part of a new discourse community know as the "blogosphere."

The popularity of blogs among adolescents has led educators to investigate ways to build blogging into class assignments. William Brescia and Michael Miller (2006) found that blogs help students learn because they increase course engagement and provide repeated exposure to content material. Richard Ferdig and Kaye Trammell (2004) identified four reasons for using blogs in the classroom: blogs help students become subject matter experts, they increase student interest and ownership of learning, they give students a legitimate chance to participate, and they provide opportunities for different perspectives both within and outside the classroom.

Blogs can play an important role in enhancing literacy. JoAnn Oravec (2002) finds that a blog can help students develop literacy by providing an online journal for personal reflection. She notes, "The blog has many dimensions that are suited to students' 'unique voices,' empowering them, and encouraging them to become more critically analytical in their thinking" (618). Some teachers use blogs as they do exit slips. Students are asked to use the class blog to reflect on what they learned that day or post any questions they still have. Blogs also encourage students to identify and defend their opinions as they develop a voice for expressing their ideas to a real audience. This makes Web logs a valuable tool in the English language arts classroom, especially when teaching students to read critically and write persuasively.

David Huffaker (2004), writing in *First Monday*, a peer-reviewed journal on the Internet, notes that blogs "provide an excellent opportunity for educators to advance literacy through storytelling and dialogue." From childhood to adulthood, as we tell stories, we develop verbal fluency. Blogging on the Internet extends verbal fluency while developing digital fluency, two important goals for our students. When investigating blogging and storytelling, Huffaker found that blogs provide arenas where self-expression and creativity are encouraged. "Its linkages to other bloggers establish the same peer-group relationships found in nonvirtual worlds" (2). Teachers can tap into student interest in blogging by creating classroom assignments that include a class blog.

For teachers who are new to blogging, Ferdig and Trammel (2004) offer some advice to get started: consider blogging yourself, visit other classroom blogs, model blogging for your students, consider an audience that goes beyond your class, and explain to students the "reach" of blogs. Teachers should provide a set of rules for blogging such as frequency, staying on topic, and number of links. It is crucial to remind students that blogs are public. Student writers need to use appropriate language when posting a comment and to avoid defamatory language. In addition, students should never give out personal information such as an address or phone number. Students should also remember that once something is posted on the Internet, the communication is irreversible. Finally, students should include citations for any work that is not their own in order to avoid copyright violations. A number of sites make it easy for teachers to set up a blog: http://edublogs.org, http://classblogmeister.com, http://funnymonkey.com, http://pbblogger.com, and https://www.Blogger.com.

Many teachers are adapting blogs because blogs "expand instructional time by providing teachers with a user-friendly online format to reinforce strategies and introduce new topics" (Colombo and Colombo 2007, 61). Addressing the concern about the availability of computers to students who need to complete a blogging assignment, Michaela and Paul Colombo (2007) acknowledge that "while all students may not have Internet connections at home, students can access and download blog files at the community library or in school computer labs or media centers during study periods, after school, and during tutorials" (61).

Another attribute of blogs that makes them appealing for classroom use is the ease with which students can return to what has been written, reflect on it, and rethink their views or their writing. Tom McHale's students at Hunterdon Central High School in New Jersey have the opportunity to do just that. Tom created a blog for his Journalism I class where he posts assignments and assessment criteria as well as student writing. There are sidebars where a visitor can access individual student blogs, which contain the stories they have completed or are currently working on. Each student's work becomes part of an individual electronic portfolio, which, when completed, is submitted for assessment. Reading these student portfolios, one can see the evolution of a piece of writing based on the comments given by others and the student's own reflections. The teacher has also included links to help his students access local and national new sources. The Journalism I blog can be found at http://central.hcrhs.k12.nj.us/mcjournalism/. Sarah Stull, a student in Tom's class, reflected on the usefulness of a Web log in journalism:

> The use of the weblog in my journalism class allowed me to review others' work and receive feedback for my own, which is essential to the development of journalism. Responses to the blog are displayed as a single thread, so one can easily pinpoint any areas of weakness from multiple responses. Links to other students' work also allow one to get an idea of how others are approaching an assignment, sparking inspiration in the reviewer. Additionally, as busy as journalists are, it's refreshing to be able to work on an assignment in a near simultaneous manner with email, an essential form of modern communication. Reviewing an email in one window. Scheduling an interview in another. Pretty simple. And, of course, the weblog eliminates the threat of lost hand-written notes. Even the most disorganized student is now liable to have a work history stored in the confines of the Web. Thus, the weblog has proved beneficial in all stages of the journalism process, for students as well as for educators.

Four teachers from South Brunswick High School in central New Jersey developed blogs to use in literature units they were teaching. April Gonzalez, Supervisor of English in South Brunswick and Advanced Placement (AP) English teacher, reported that one reason the group of teachers turned to blogs was because they ran out of time during Socratic Seminar class discussions. Blogs offered a way to extend the class discussions, a way for students to continue sharing ideas outside the classroom. Before introducing a blog to her AP English class, April surveyed the students and found that only 10 to 13 percent of them reported blogging previously, and none had done so for academic purposes. She decided to create a blog that could be visited by invitation only—that is, it was not open to people outside her class. She also gave the students pseudonyms because she felt they would be more willing to share ideas under another name. Before beginning a class blog, April showed her students sample blogs. She found that the class blog was very successful. It promoted serious literary discussions beyond the classroom. In addition, she noted that the students enjoyed and valued the experience. Students reported that reading and writing the blog didn't feel like homework. One student commented that when the blog stopped, she felt her voice was taken away. This student verbalized what many others felt about the blog: it gave them a place to express freely their ideas to a real audience that listened. It gave them a voice.

Stephanie Bogetti, a ninth-grade English teacher in South Brunswick, used blogging when her students were studying Shakespeare's *Romeo and Juliet*. Stephanie gave her students pseudonyms based on major and minor characters in the play. She began the unit by modeling blogging under the pseudonym "Shakespeare." Stephanie took her students to the computer lab for their first assignment and asked them to post a comment as the character they were assigned. This involved researching the character of their pseudonym and writing a paragraph introducing the character to peer bloggers. The student bloggers also had to respond to the blog entry of one other character, thus giving them initial practice in posting and commenting on a blog. Stephanie gave her students some basic guidelines for using the blog. These included "no trash talking as character to character, and no IM [instant messaging] language." She also discussed plagiarism with the class and emphasized the importance of posting only original work. Students were then instructed to blog after reading each act of *Romeo and Juliet*. They had specific topics to focus on, including imagery and important lines. The students were also asked to post any questions they had and to respond to any questions their peers raised.

Based on her observations of student comments and questions, as well as on their final written paper, Stephanie found that her students' comprehension improved when reading *Romeo and Juliet*. The blogging helped them make sense of the difficult language and challenging plot developments. Near the end of the unit, Stephanie assigned a paper on who was to blame for the outcome at the end of the play. She found that the students had great ideas and support for their papers based on the blogging they had done. Another assignment asked students to write original sonnets and post them on the blog for feedback. In addition to the success she saw with reading and writing, Stephanie also noticed that when blogging was included, her students completed homework more often than they did when blogging was not part of the assignment. Her suggestions for doing a class blog next time include limiting comments to two each per session and using a rubric for blogging. Examples of rubrics for assessing blogs can be found online by typing "rubric for blogs" into a search engine. Rubrics online can be modified to fit specific class needs or used as posted.

A colleague of Stephanie, Janelle Duryea-Lojko, introduced blogging to her freshmen in an English I Honors class that was studying Charles Dickens' *A Tale of Two Cities*. Janelle felt that blogging might help this class because most of the students were hesitant to speak up. Also, blogging gave students more time to process new ideas and then comment on them. Setting up a blog for the first time, she admitted, was time-consuming, but the fact that she was working collaboratively with other teachers helped. She found that more students were willing to voice their observations and opinions on the class blog than were willing to do so in a class discussion.

A fourth teacher from South Brunswick High School, Shauna Beardslee, found that her students took to the technology and went beyond it. The comments they made on the blog filtered into class and improved the literature discussions. Jim Burke (2007) calls this "threaded discussions." He noted that in class discussions, his students began to refer to comments that were made outside of class on the online forum (161). Shauna also found that the blog entries and the class discussions based on them helped students write better literary analysis papers. For example, she saw students improve in their ability to embed quotations. Students claimed that seeing other student models on the blog helped them write better.

All four teachers who worked with class blogs at South Brunswick High School agree that if a teacher were to check each blog entry daily for four or five classes, the process would be unmanageable. Therefore, they suggest teachers check blogs periodically. Students are informed that the teacher will be reading the blogs, but they do not know when these checks will occur. The teachers also found that they can get a sense of what the students are writing and thinking by quickly skimming the blogs. These teachers also find it easier to start by introducing a class blog with just one class if a teacher is new to the process. After teachers become familiar with using a blog, they can have students from different class periods communicate with each other by using a common blog site.

Most English language arts blogs are used in one of four ways: for posting assignments and rubrics, for conducting peer-to-peer discussions, for receiving feedback on posted student work, and for creating a collaborative piece of writing. All four ways to use blogs have potential for differentiating instruction.

When the teacher uses a blog for posting assignments, the assignments can be differentiated. Links can be included that take students to different sites for specific instructions or for different resources. By using different links, students can also view rubrics that are specific to their assignments. Peer-to-peer literature discussions can be differentiated by aligning specific discussion prompts with the texts the students are reading. Giving feedback on student work is differentiated by the uniqueness of each piece posted. Teachers can direct the peer feedback by posting guidelines or offering prompts for students to respond to. In addition, students can ask for the specific type of feedback they want. Finally, blogs can be used to create a collaborative piece of writing by having each student add content and revise what has been posted. A planning guide for tiered blogging tasks is presented in Figure 8–3. Figure 8–4 contains the tiered blogging assignments.

Wikis and Differentiated Instruction

A wiki is "a website that allows readers, users, and writers to easily contribute content or edit existing content that is viewable online" (Kajder 2007, 223). Although wikis be can be used like blogs, there are some basic differences between blogs and wikis. Visitors to blogs can read comments and add to them, but they cannot change what is already posted. Visitors to most wiki sites can change the content by clicking an edit button. In addition, blogs tend to contain opinions and observations, while wikis generally contain facts and information. The term *wiki* is said to come from the Hawaiian word for *fast* or *quickly*. Wikis are websites that can quickly and easily be constructed and accessed.

Although most wikis found online are open to the public and anyone can edit the content, teachers and students can create wiki pages that require a password. For these wikis, anyone can view the wiki, but in order to edit it, the visitor has to log on and use a password. Because wikis have records of the changes made by different users, teachers can see which students are contributing and the changes they make. Teachers have found www.wikispaces.com, www.wetpaint.com, and http://pbworks.com helpful for establishing class wikis. Both PBworks and Wetpaint allow teachers to create password-protected wikis.

The most famous wiki is Wikipedia (http://wikipedia.org), an online collaborative encyclopedia. Michele Cooke-Andresen, a geology professor at the

Figure 8–3

Planning Guide for Blogging and Tiered Assignment

Course Title and Level: Grade 8 Language Arts

Unit: Enhancing Communication: Establishing a Class Blog

Essential Questions

How can blogs enhance communication in a classroom?

Why might students feel freer to express their ideas on a blog?

How can students take ownership of a class blog?

Unit-Specific Questions

How can students learn about blogging?

How do students create and maintain a blog?

What are some benefits of a classroom blog?

How does having a rubric enhance a classroom blog?

Knowledge/Skills

Students will understand how blogs work.

Students will know how to blog (how to make a new entry and respond to a posted message).

Students will understand how to assess blogs.

Students will know how to create a rubric.

Modes of Differentiation Used

Content: Differentiate content by readiness level.

Process: Differentiate time frame and teacher support by readiness level.

Based on (readiness, interests, learning styles)

Readiness

Strategy: tiered tasks

Figure 8–4

Tiered Blogging Tasks

Note to teacher: Students are assigned a tier based on their experience and comfort with blogging. Teachers can find examples of classroom blogs online. This is an assignment in which the tech-savvy students in class can really excel.

Tier One

You will be given the site of a classroom blog to visit. When you visit the site, identify what the content is, who the bloggers are, and what types of comments are made. After you have read the blog, write a brief review of the blog to present to your classmates. Include your thoughts on the how a class blog could be used in your class.

Tier Two

Review two blogging rubrics found online. Compare the two, identifying what you like about each and what you would change. Working in small groups, create a rubric for your class blog. You need to consult with your teacher as you construct the rubric. Consider the goals for blogging in your class and how you can make the rubric unique for your class.

Tier Three

Visit at least two English language arts class blog sites. Next, working in a group, design a blog for your class. Consider the purpose of the blog and how it will be maintained. Also decide if it will include links to other sources and what they should be. You need to consult with your teacher as you develop the blog.

University of Massachusetts, had her students visit the Wikipedia website to check on the information presented about a particular landslide they were studying. Then, based on what they had learned about the landslide, the students edited any misinformation or incomplete entries. Similar activities could be included in an English language arts class. A common assignment for middle and high school students is to research the life of a famous author. Although the students are not experts in literary history, they can still compare their findings to what is posted on Wikipedia. This assignment has multiple benefits that go beyond reading and writing: first, it directs students to go beyond Wikipedia for research; second, it shows them that not all entries on Wikipedia are correct or complete; and third, it reinforces comparative thinking. In addition, the assignment is easily differentiated by allowing students to select the authors they want to research.

Wikis are a way for students to share their ideas, writings, and images. Sara Kajder (2007) sees wikis as "collaborative writing places in that [students] can read, write, and edit a shared document" (224). She included a wiki in her class when her students were studying Albert Camus' *The Stranger*. Recognizing that *The Stranger* is a challenging text and seeing that her students immediately reached for CliffsNotes before they had even begun reading the text, Kajder asked her students to create a reader's guide for the novel. Using the http://wikibooks.org website, students set up an annotated text as they read the book. By the end of the unit, the class had created a study guide that was multimodal and was being visited by people from other parts of the country daily. Kajder notes that knowing others were really reading their guide motivated the students to complete the project. Wikis, she concludes, help connect students to a larger community of readers (2007, 223–24). Assignments such as this one lend themselves to differentiating instruction. Students, working alone or in small groups, could be responsible for different parts of the reader's guide. For example, students could work on the background of the novel, chapter summaries, literary devices, and the author's biography. All students could be involved in generating questions for discussion.

"British Romanticism" is a class wiki created by Damian Bariexca's Major British Writers class in the spring of 2007 at Hunterdon Central Regional High School in New Jersey. Damian's goal was to have his students not only research and present information, but also create a document that could be used as a resource by other students. In addition, he wanted to create an assignment that was authentic. During this two-week project, working in groups of three or four, students collaboratively composed a wiki that presents a humanities-based overview of the British Romantic period. The student groups had to complete four parts of a task: conduct research on the Romantic period in Britain in one of three areas: poetry, visual art, and music; collaboratively compose a 500- to 700-word article on one of the three areas; conduct a detailed critical analysis of two works of the time period and provide complete documentation for all sources. Giving the students choice in the topics they researched and reported on built differentiated instruction into the wiki project. Damian reports that 99 percent of the feedback he received from his students was positive. In an email message to the authors on November 18, 2008, Damian stated, "More than perhaps any other assignment this year, the students really took ownership of this project." Many students commented on this being the most practical work they have done in an English class in high school. The students believed that this work was practical because they were able to track site traffic. Damian observed that the students "would really get excited when we got a visitor from a new state, country, or continent. It allowed them to feel that there was some greater purpose to their work than just demonstrating to me that they knew how to do research." The British Romantic Period project and other class wiki projects created by Damian share a common goal of getting "kids to contribute to an organic growing body of knowledge, and then share that knowledge with the rest of the world."

Carrie Costello has created a paperless journalism class at Kennett High School in North Conway, New Hampshire, using Web 2.0 applications—what she refers to as the "big four" applications: PBworks, Writeboard, Delicious, and Edublog.

PBworks is the site where the journalism students begin their day. Carrie sees PBworks as the launching pad for the class. Students go to that site when they log on for the day. This website is truly "one-stop shopping" because it is a well-organized home for all the class resources. There are folders for class notes, story ideas, spreadsheets that track peer feedback, pictures, and "virtual handouts." There are links in the sidebar to the other three of the big four sites: Writeboard, Delicious, and Edublog. Anyone who has been invited to the "community" of the wiki can leave comments on any page, contribute content, and make changes to any page. The teacher is the administrator of the wiki, and she receives an email any time anything changes on the wiki.

Writeboard is where the students post all of their writing. They can either copy and paste their writing from a word-processing document or type right into the "writeboard," which is like a blank piece of paper. This application tracks any changes to the writing and saves them as different versions. This way, the students can revisit any incarnation of the piece of writing, and it provides the teacher with a running record when students have worked on their articles and shows how much revising they have done over the life of the piece. After the Writeboard for the article is created, the students link it to the social bookmarking page of the class. The article is then only two clicks away. The documents are password protected, so they are not viewable by the public. Students can access them through a common password for the class that is used for all of applications.

Delicious (formerly del.icio.us) is a social bookmarking site where people bookmark their favorite websites in a public fashion. Carrie has established an account for the class. Their page is basically a series of links that are important to the functioning of the class. This includes links to online news sources such as the *New York Times* and journalism resources such as *Poynter Online.* There is also a link to every article that the students have created in Writeboard and to websites that Carrie uses to teach minilessons to the class, such as "The Society of Professional Journalists' Code of Ethics." In addition, Carrie bookmarks articles that she wants the students to read, and the students are able to add a bookmark for anything they come across that might be pertinent to the class.

Edublogs is a home for blogs created by those in the world of education. The students search online news sources each Wednesday for breaking stories and ideas for new articles. Once the students find an article that interests them, they blog a summary of the article, relate it to a possible story for class publication, and provide a link to the actual article. On Thursdays, Carrie projects the blog onto a screen, the students gather in the front of the room, and they present and discuss their story ideas. The managing editor takes notes on the discussion and saves them to a special folder in the wiki.edublogs. Carrie encourages her students to write at their own pace and produce as much as they can. Because the class publication is a magazine, the deadlines are looser than those of a newspaper.

Carrie found that using these Web applications has made the students work more collaboratively and write better because they are writing and receiving feedback daily from their teacher and their peers. The journalism wiki can be viewed at http://khsjournalism.pbworks.com/.

The examples presented here are but a few of the ways wikis and related technology can be used in English language arts classrooms. In addition to reader's guides, historical material, and analyses of texts, class wikis can be used for creating a glossary, presenting annotated vocabulary lists, posting student projects and writings, presenting discussion questions, and posting book and film reviews. All of these uses of wikis provide opportunities to differentiate instruction.

WebQuests and Differentiated Instruction

Although not new, WebQuests remain a powerful use of technology in the classroom. The earliest WebQuest model for using the Internet in the classroom was developed at San Diego State University by Bernie Dodge in the mid 1990s. Dodge wanted to create a tool for students so that their research could focus on using information, not finding it. It remains a useful model for cooperative and independent work today. In addition, WebQuests continue to be popular with students. According to Sara Kajder (2003), "The WebQuest is both a research tool and an active, engaging learning activity" (77).

WebQuests are inquiry-based activities in which some or all of the information that learners interact with comes from resources on the Internet (Dodge 1995). WebQuests are scaffolded experiences, with the teacher supplying links on the Internet that students are to access while engaging in authentic tasks. WebQuests support student-centered learning because, although the teacher sets up the task and the links for students to pursue, the students conduct the research and draw conclusions based on that research. "The WebQuest demands that the teacher act as a facilitator, designing the learning environment and task for students while ultimately charging them with responsibility for their own learning" (Kajder 2003, 78). Kajder's description of a WebQuest defines a constructivist approach to learning. As students pursue a WebQuest, they are creating meaning and constructing knowledge.

The best WebQuests go beyond reporting to having students "transform newly acquired information into a more sophisticated understanding" (March 2004, 43).

Conducting a WebQuest requires thinking that incorporates the higher-level processes identified in Bloom's Taxonomy (1956). Open-ended questions or debatable topics for students to pursue support higher-level thinking and true learning. For example, when studying Carl Hiaasen's *Hoot* in a middle school language arts class, teachers can ask their students, "How does a community decide when it is environmentally inappropriate to construct new buildings?" Teachers can then assign specific roles based on the characters in the book and ask the students to investigate and present their findings from the point of view of their character in the book. Another way to initiate a WebQuest in both middle and high school English language arts classes is to ask students to consider the following questions: What makes a work of literature a classic? Should the text we are reading be considered a classic? Should it be required reading in the curriculum? What books that you consider classics should be in our curriculum? After researching what makes a classic and what constitutes the literary canon, students may answer the questions from their own point of view or from the point of view of a parent or educator.

English language arts teachers can find many prepared WebQuests on different Internet sites. As with anything found on the Internet, teachers need to evaluate the WebQuests carefully. Teachers should determine if the WebQuest moves learning beyond simple reporting. There are many good WebQuests that teachers can use directly in their classrooms and others that teachers may need to adapt so that they better fit the class goals and the needs of the students. A helpful place to begin looking at WebQuests that have already been created is http://bestwebquests.com. This website is maintained by Tom March, who worked with Bernie Dodge on the original WebQuest model. The site contains many WebQuest examples for middle and high school English language arts teachers. In addition to traditional literary topics, there are WebQuests that explore controversial issues that can be used for classroom debate or writing topics. All WebQuests on this site have been carefully evaluated before being posted.

To develop their own WebQuests, teachers can follow a basic template of the components of a WebQuest: introduction, task, information resources, process, evaluation, and conclusion. Nancy Shanklin (2008) further explains each of these sections (49). The introduction asks a question or poses a problem to introduce the topic. The teacher explains the task, what she wants the students to do, and indicates whether it is to be an individual or group task. The information resources section lists the websites the teacher has identified. The teacher can assign roles in the process section, if applicable, and give specific directions for completing the task. In the evaluation section, the students are told how they will be evaluated if, for example, a rubric will be used. The criteria for evaluation should be explained in this section. The conclusion should include what students have learned as a result of engaging in this WebQuest. The conclusion can be written as leading or essential questions and, as such, be identified early in the planning process. The step-by-step design process created by Bernie Dodge can be accessed online by going to the San Diego State University WebQuest website: http://webquest.sdu.edu. Another site that can help teachers develop WebQuests is the Web resources section at www.readwritethink.org.

WebQuests support differentiated instruction because they can be designed based on student readiness and interests and can be conducted as a group or individual inquiry. When designing a WebQuest based on readiness levels, the teacher can direct students to reading materials that require different levels of reading readiness. As Nancy Shanklin notes, "In a sense, WebQuests become essentially Web-based 'text sets'" (2008, 48). Student interest can also play an important role when deciding on a WebQuest. Tom March (2004) notes, "The best way to address attention and relevance is to choose a topic that students find compelling and then create an authentic learning task to fit it" (44). If students are interested in a topic, they are more motivated to follow a project through to completion. WebQuests can also be differentiated by varying the scaffolding, the amount and type of support the teacher provides, based on each student's experience with conducting research and using the Internet. Advanced students, those who are already familiar with WebQuests, can design their own WebQuests to share with their classmates. A number of rubrics for assessing WebQuests can be found on the Internet. Before students begin creating their own WebQuests, they should review the attributes listed on sample rubrics.

Wilfredo Rivera, an English teacher at South Brunswick High School in New Jersey, has created a WebQuest for a unit on Willa Cather's novel, *My Antonia*. Before reading the novel, instead of giving his tenth-grade students the background information about Cather's life and prairie life, Wilfredo asked his students to discover this information for themselves by conducting a WebQuest. For each website they visit, students must complete worksheets prepared by Wilfredo. After visiting the Willa Cather website (www.willacather.org), students list important facts about the author's life and print out pictures of Cather, her childhood home, and her hometown. After visiting a website for the setting of the novel, Red Cloud, Nebraska (www.redcloudnebraska.com), students describe what Red Cloud is like and what it is known for. The next part of the WebQuest takes students beyond simple identification to making inferences and drawing conclusions. At www.edc.org/CCT/PMA/prairie/index.html, students learn what brought people to the prairie, what the environment was like, and then students consider why people might have decided to leave the prairie. Next, the students identify a picture on the website that best reflects their image of prairie life and write a paragraph stating why they chose the picture. A fourth website is connected to the theme of the novel, the American Dream. Students are asked to go to the Web page at www.memory.loc.gov/learn/lessons/97/dream/task.html. After reading over the dreams at this site, the students each write a paragraph explaining which dream they agree with the most. The next part of the WebQuest takes the students to a website on pioneers, www.library.thinkquest.org. After viewing this site, students answer questions about traveling to the frontier and some of the trails pioneers used. The next website is related to a quotation from the book. Students are instructed to go to google.com and type in the Latin phrase "Optima Dies . . . prima fugit." The students then answer the question, "What does this phrase mean?" Finally, after going to the website http://user.rcn.com/deeds/homestead, students are asked to explain the Homestead Act of 1862. When the students have completed this WebQuest, they construct background knowledge on the author's life, the setting, and the issues facing settlers who moved to the prairie. In addition, they are introduced to a theme that they will encounter in the novel. The WebQuest is a highly engaging prereading research assignment that builds student knowledge about prairie life and the life of the author before reading the novel.

The new literacies are multimodal and cover a range of technologies. Many of our students are at different ends of the spectrum when it comes to knowledge of and comfort with technology. The multimodal tasks presented on the choice board in Figure 8–5 represent a range of technology. Students who are not adept at using technology or do not have access to it readily may choose a low-tech task

Figure 8–5

Multimodal Choice Board

Directions for teachers: Students may work alone, in pairs, or in small groups. They may complete one task or three in a row. You may adjust the directions to fit the needs of your class.

Draw illustrations for three key events in the novel or play you read.	Create a video or podcast of three key scenes in the novel or play you read.	Design a cover for a new edition of the novel or play you read. You may prepare the cover in print or digitalized form.
Create a digitalized presentation (such as a PowerPoint) of the theme, setting, and plot of the novel or play you read.	*Free Choice Square* Students suggest their own tasks. The tasks need to contain some multimodal element and need to be cleared with the teacher.	Create a visual collage that incorporates key quotations and portrays the theme of the novel or play you read. This collage may be in print or digitalized form.
Select three key scenes from the novel or play you read and make a music CD for each scene. The music you select should reflect the mood of the scene.	Select three key events in the novel or play you read and create a series of graphic novel panels for each event chosen.	Present a WebQuest that contains at least six hypertext links a reader can access to learn more about the author as well as the time and place in which the novel or play is set.

such as drawing a book cover. More technologically advanced students may opt to create a WebQuest or a PowerPoint presentation.

The key to using the new literacies in the classroom is to understand that the students' expertise with them is also changing. All students need to be literate members of an increasingly technological world, but they learn in diverse ways and are at different places on the technological learning curve. As with other strategies that support differentiated learning, teachers need to meet students where they are and provide scaffolded experiences to move them forward in their learning.

Adolescent Literacy and Differentiated Instruction Beyond the English Classroom

9

Literacy does not stop at the English language arts classroom door; therefore, literacy instruction should not stop there, especially as content-specific texts make specific demands on adolescent readers. As noted in the National Council of Teachers of English "Adolescent Literacy" report (2007), teachers across the curriculum need to "demystify content-specific literacy practices" (1). Reading a math textbook, for example, is not the same as reading a social studies textbook. Although general reading strategies, such as previewing a chapter or activating prior knowledge, cut across all content areas, reading assignments in each academic subject have unique text structure features and vocabularies.

"Why can't these students read the textbook?" is a common complaint heard in faculty rooms across the country. This is frequently followed by, "You're the English teacher; I thought your job was to teach them to read." The answer to the first question is, "Most students probably can read the textbook with the appropriate help." The answer to the second question is, "It is every teacher's job to help students read better."

In the 1970s, a popular phrase in middle and secondary school was, "Every teacher is a reading teacher." With the demands of high-stakes tests that focus on content knowledge, subject area teachers are concerned that they do not have enough time to teach their content, let alone teach reading. This concern is a misinterpretation of what is meant by all teachers being responsible for teaching reading. Teaching reading in the content areas does not mean teaching students the basics of reading, such as word attack skills or phonics. It means modeling strategies for how to approach subject-specific textbooks and providing scaffolded support as students approach these texts for the first time. It means employing prereading strategies, such as those discussed in Chapter 4, to introduce the topic and help students connect new information with what they already know. It means introducing key vocabulary words and content-specific terminology before reading so that students can better comprehend the information in the text when they encounter the new words and concepts. It also means asking the students to do something with the text while they are reading. Reader-text interaction is an important part of the reading process. If students are asked to think about and respond to the text in some way, they cannot "pretend" to have read it. For example, students can be asked to write down questions they have about a specific part of the text or to keep a double-entry journal on the reading selection.

Reading across the curriculum focuses on reading to learn. When content area teachers take the time to demonstrate how to approach and respond to a text, they are helping their students learn the subject matter better.

English language arts teachers can help their colleagues by modeling reading strategies, especially textbook reading strategies, for their peers. This can be done at department meetings, at faculty meetings, or on professional development days. English language arts teachers can also offer advice and point peers to resources that will help them. A number of general and content-specific texts on reading across the curriculum are readily available. An effective staff development program is to choose one of these texts and form a professional book study group that meets periodically to read and discuss the book.

Content area teachers have also voiced concerns about teaching writing. Although the writing across the curriculum movement has gained more acceptance than reading across the curriculum over the past twenty years, it still needs to be bolstered. Teachers need to be reminded that there are different types of writing. Not all writing has to go through the entire writing process that is presented in Chapter 5. The full writing process is generally employed when composing a formal piece of writing, such as an essay or written report. Short, writing-to-learn activities can be used in the classroom or assigned for homework. This type of writing assignment asks students to write about what they have read or reflect on their own learning processes. In addition, there are times when content area teachers need to assign timed, writing-on-demand tasks. These tasks are important for students to practice before they take standardized tests. The tasks also help prepare students for essay exams.

Differentiated Instruction Across the Curriculum

Concerning differentiating literacy across the curriculum, the same strategies that support literacy in the English language arts classroom can be applied to all content areas. Choice boards, tiered assignments, and learning stations, for example, can be used across the curriculum. In addition, a number of websites are available for differentiating lessons in specific content areas, such as math, social studies, and world languages. These can be located by doing a search on the Internet. A popular site that offers examples for tiering or layering lessons across the curriculum is Kathie Nunley's website at www.help4teachers.com.

As with reading and writing across the curriculum, English language arts teachers can help their colleagues understand and develop differentiated lessons by sharing successful models. Just remember that, as with any new practice, it is best to start small. Colleagues may not be willing to jump right into differentiated instruction but may be willing to try one strategy or to start with differentiating a homework assignment. Sharing examples and discussing them with peers is the best way to help others accept any new teaching practice.

Adolescent Literacy and Differentiated Instruction Outside of School

The world outside of school offers endless opportunities for literacy development and differentiated instruction. Employers and representatives from professional and community organizations are often willing to visit schools to share their observations on how important good literacy skills are to success in business and community service. Many such organizations also offer "how-to" presentations for middle and secondary students. Representatives from these organizations can speak on a range of topics from how to write an effective police report to how to behave on a job interview.

Community groups and businesses can provide a wonderful source of mentors for students. Because these mentors represent diverse backgrounds and interests, they can provide role models that may not be available within the school. They also can motivate adolescents by mentoring them one-on-one or in small groups. Often mentors can connect with students by sharing a common interest with them, applying differentiation based on interests.

In addition, many professional and community organizations sponsor writing and speaking competitions. Representatives of the organizations can share with students the standards on which the contests will be judged. For writing contests, they can also provide winning sample essays or poems. Seeing what other students have produced can be highly motivating.

Another way to reinforce literacy based on shared interests is to help students establish book groups as after-school or outside-of-school clubs. Adolescent book groups can be constructed in different ways, based, for example, on themes, authors, or genres. Some of the most popular adolescent book groups outside of school focus on specific genres: science fiction, horror, and graphic novels.

A variation on book groups is a film group. Both book groups and film groups can be official school activities or clubs, or they can be completely student-directed and meet away from the school campus. Students who have a genuine interest in a book are more likely to read it carefully if they know they will be talking about it with their friends. A similar thing happens with movies. If students know they are going to get together afterward to talk about the movie, they pay closer attention to the plot and the filming techniques. In both cases, books and films, the more adolescents talk with others about their observations, the better they understand what they have just read or seen.

Inside or outside the classroom, adolescents are using their literacy skills every day to communicate their thoughts and feelings in diverse settings. When teachers can provide real audiences for these communications, student engagement and motivation increase. The more adolescents are engaged, the more they are willing to practice the skills and strategies they are learning. The more they practice, the better they get.

Literacy is crucial to all learning and to all communication within as well as beyond the English language arts classroom. Adolescents need to be taught in environments that support the individual nature of their learning and celebrate their strengths. Adolescents benefit from literacy instruction throughout the high school years, yet not all adolescents need the same amount or type of instruction and support. The examples presented throughout this text provide a starting point to help teachers meet the challenge of helping diverse learners succeed in school and beyond.

Glossary

The widespread dissemination of the idea and ideals of differentiated instruction over the past ten years has led to some confusion with regard to definitions of terms and concepts. For example, *anchor activities* to some means those ideas recorded on large paper or anchor charts during reading instruction. Others view *anchor activities* as the work students do when they enter the classroom that some teachers call "bell work," "sponge activities," or "do nows." Additionally, the term *anchor* is used in many secondary English classrooms to relate to writing samples that exemplify characteristics of a certain grading score. However, for differentiated instruction, the term *anchor activities* refers to those assignments that the students work on when they are finished with the day's regular work. The following glossary offers definitions of terms that are referenced in the rest of this book. This glossary is provided to minimize confusion and to promote clarity of understanding.

Anchor Activities Anchor activities are activities that students can work on when they finish an assignment before their classmates or when they have free time, for example, when they are waiting for a conference with the teacher or a peer. Anchor activities are not busywork; they are meaningful activities that give the students practice in applying the skills and concepts they have learned. Anchor activities need to be assignments that students can work on independently and that can be taken up and put down without interruption. These activities are important in the differentiated classroom because they support a basic tenet that in such a classroom, learning is never done or finished. They also reinforce the idea that learners are responsible for their own achievement. For example, reading an "anchor activity" newspaper article on the events in Birmingham during the 1960s serves to further enlighten a student's understanding of *The Watsons Go to Birmingham*.

Blog   *Blog* is the common name for a Web log, an electronic bulletin board or journal. Blogs are accessible on the Internet where students can communicate with each other. Teachers can create class blogs where students can post questions or continue discussions outside the classroom. Most classroom blogs are password-protected.

Curriculum Compacting   Compacting allows students to be accelerated based on readiness. There are times when students do not need to learn everything planned for a unit because they already know some, if not all, of the material being studied. When teachers begin a unit, they first ascertain what prior knowledge their students possess. If a student already knows much of the material, the teacher can compact the curriculum. First, the teacher gives a test or other form of preassessment to be assured that the student knows the material. Next, the teacher develops a plan of study for this student that goes beyond the basics of the unit to an investigation or application of the main concepts or skills being studied. In any given unit, only part of the information and skills may be new for some students. The curriculum can be compacted in the areas the students know, but they participate with the rest of the class in other areas of the unit.

E-books or Digital Books   E-books are electronic versions of printed texts. They can be read on a computer or on an e-book reading device. One advantage that e-books have over printed texts is hyperlinks that can take the reader immediately to related sources.

Flexible Grouping   Flexible grouping is fundamental to differentiated instruction classrooms. In flexible grouping, students move into and out of groups either by choice or by teacher assignment. Students may be grouped based on the same interests or readiness or learning styles, or they may work in a group that is mixed. By using flexible grouping, students work with many different classmates during a unit of study, because groups do not stay the same for a long period of time.

Graphic Novels and Mangas   Graphic novels tell stories by combining text and graphics, much like a sophisticated comic book. *Mangas* are the Japanese form of graphic novels. Although their content is similar, *mangas* are read from the back to the front, from right to left. Graphic novels go beyond most comic books by presenting intricate narrative plot structures and fully developed characters. But graphic novels do not have to be narratives. There are also graphic forms of biographies, autobiographies, and information texts.

Independent Study and Learning Contracts   Independent study gives students the opportunity to pursue in depth something they want to know more about. Independent study can be offered to students who wish to investigate a subject in which they have a sincere interest or to those who have already mastered the unit's content and are ready to pursue advanced information and concepts. Independent study begins with the teacher and student identifying an area and agreeing on a plan, timeline, and final product. Independent study projects can be completed during the class time if the student has "compacted" out of the unit or part of the unit, or the projects can be completed outside of the class during the student's own time. Most independent projects include a learning contract, a formal agreement between the teacher and the student. Learning contracts contain goals, timelines, and a plan for assessing the final product.

Learning Stations   Stations are differentiated activities that can be based on readiness, interests, learning styles or any combination of the three. Learning stations differ from learning centers in that they are created for a particular assignment or unit of study and are not permanent work areas in the classroom. Students may have free choice in selecting stations or they may be assigned. The classroom teacher differentiates stations by deciding how much choice to allow and which stations to require. Stations can be differentiated by giving students separate sets of instructions, identifying the stations they need to complete.

Learning Styles A learning style or learning preference refers to a person's preferred way of receiving and processing information. People learn in different ways. There are many models of learning styles, the most popular being Howard Gardner's multiple intelligence theory (1983). Teachers can develop assignments and assessments based on student differences in learning styles in order to maximize learning.

Literacy *Literacy* refers to multiple forms of symbolic communication, such as reading, writing, speaking, listening, or viewing. Multimodal and the new literacies expand the definition of literacy to include integrated media and digital forms of communication.

Literature Circles Literature circles support differentiation because of their emphasis on student choice and the use of multiple texts to support differentiation. Although there are different models for using literature circles, Harvey Daniels (2002) developed a model that is widely used in English classes. Literature circles combine cooperative learning and independent reading. Students select the work they wish to read and discuss. They may select the work from a teacher-prepared list or from outside texts. Literature circle groups meet for a specified period of time to discuss a book, poem, short story, or article read in common. In his original model, Daniels assigns specific roles to each member of the group. These roles often include: discussion director, literary luminary, connector, illustrator, word master, and character captain. The roles rotate each time the group meets. By using literature circles in the class, an English teacher can offer a range of titles for the students to read and can offer learners a variety of interpretive experiences and roles.

Multimodal *Multimodal* refers to material accessed or created in more than one mode. Multimodal texts use more than one mode to communicate meaning, for example, images and printed text. Graphic novels and films are two examples of multimodal texts.

Multiple Intelligences Multiple intelligence theory is a theory of cognitive functioning—how we process information. Multiple intelligence theory suggests that no one set of teaching strategies works best for all students all the time. Students have different proclivities in the different intelligences. Therefore, teachers need to use a range of teaching strategies within a unit of study. No intelligence exits all by itself; they all work together. Most people have a preference for one or more intelligences over others. Howard Gardner has identified eight intelligences: linguistic, logical-mathematical, spatial, interpersonal, intrapersonal, naturalist, bodily-kinesthetic, and musical (1993).

Performance Assessments Performance assessments, also known as authentic assessments, provide students with the opportunity to demonstrate their learning through a variety of products in different modes. For this reason, performance assessments can support differentiation based on both readiness and learning styles. Insofar as possible, performance assessments try to duplicate activities that people actually do in the world outside of school. Rubrics or scoring guides accompany performance assessments so students can have a clear understanding of how their products will be assessed. Performance assessments may be small activities within or at the end of a classroom unit, or they can be major course requirements across the school.

Podcast Podcasts are play-on-demand digital audio or visual files that can be distributed over the Internet. Podcasts can be accessed by a personal computer or downloaded to a portable MP3 player. They can also be burned onto a CD. Like other new literacies media, they integrate reading, writing, speaking, and listening. Students can listen to or view professionally produced podcasts or they can create their own.

Reading Workshop Reading workshop is based on the belief that students learn to read by reading. In a reading workshop, students read independently and then share their responses. Students frequently keep reading response journals. Novels are usually the vehicle for this type of workshop.

Socratic Seminar Socratic Seminar is a discussion strategy that emphasizes thoughtful dialogue among the students without teacher intervention. It is based on the Socratic questioning model adapted for classrooms by Mortimer Adler of the *Paideia Proposal* (1982). Classroom teachers have developed variations on Socratic Seminar. In one model, all students sit in a circle and participate in an open-ended discussion. The teacher serves as the moderator and may also pose the questions to be discussed. Another variation on this model is to have the students pose the questions. Some teachers ask students to prepare open-ended questions ahead of time for the discussion. In a second configuration, students sit in two concentric circles, with the inner circle discussing a topic or text and the outer circle observing (Ball and Brewer 2000). Halfway through the discussion, the two circles exchange places. A variation on this second model is to have the students in the outer circle give feedback to the students in the inner circle.

Tic-Tac-Toe and Choice Boards   Classroom teachers have found using the tic-tac-toe and choice boards to be a positive way to differentiate assignments. The assignments on the board may be arranged by rows and columns representing degree of difficulty or by rows and columns representing learning preferences. Students must complete a tic-tac-toe board by selecting and completing three assignments in a row by the end of the unit. A choice board is similar to a tic-tac-toe board, but the students can choose which assignments they wish to complete, not necessarily three in a row.

Tiered Assignments   Tiered assignments are used when teachers want "to ensure that students with different learning needs work with the same essential ideas and use the same key skills" (Tomlinson 1993, 83). Tiered assignments are based on differences in readiness levels. The goals, the enduring understandings, and the essential questions remain the same, but the level of complexity of the tasks varies. Students who demonstrate an advanced knowledge of the concept or skill being addressed can be asked to complete tasks at a higher level of complexity or abstraction. Students who struggle to learn the basics can be asked to complete a less complex and more concrete task.

WebQuest   A WebQuest is an inquiry-based activity designed by teachers to help students effectively negotiate the Internet for a teacher-assigned or student-selected topic. When creating WebQuests, the teacher predetermines Internet links that are connected to the agreed-upon topic. Because teachers predetermine the Internet links, WebQuests are a good introduction to research using the World Wide Web. They also help students avoid accessing inappropriate material. WebQuests support differentiated instruction because they can be based on student readiness and interest and can be conducted as a group or an individual inquiry.

Wiki A wiki is "a website that allows readers, users, and writers easily to contribute content or edit existing content that is viewable online" (Kajder 2007, 223). Visitors to blogs can read comments and add to them, but they cannot change what is already posted, but visitors to most wiki sites can change the content by clicking an edit button. Although most wikis found online are open to the public and anyone can edit the content, teachers and students can create wiki pages that require a password.

Writing Workshop Writing workshop is based on a process approach to writing. Students meet in small groups to share their writing and receive feedback from their peers. Writing workshop allows students to work on different parts of the writing process at the same time. For example, some students may prewrite on a topic while other students meet in peer groups to give and receive feedback on drafts that have been completed.

Book Study Questions

Learning is inherently social. Though sometimes we feel isolated as teachers, most of us know the benefits of taking time to engage with colleagues. It is in these conversations, or "teacher talk" as Regie Routman (1991) calls it, that we find our own ideas clarified and enriched. This is particularly true when new ideas, such as Response to Intervention, arise in education. Although there are many ways to structure a study group, it is most important to foster a climate in which teachers feel free and safe to participate in the ongoing conversations and exchange of ideas. Other guidelines can make book study more productive. Here are a few things you might consider. In addition to using these questions for discussion groups with practicing teachers, professors can use these questions to help preservice and student teachers understand and apply differentiated instruction with adolescent learners.

Watch Group Size

You may want to kick off discussion with a general question and then break into smaller groups. Often the optimal number is four or six to ensure there is time for all to exchange ideas. The larger group can reassemble at the end to debrief.

Use Study Questions

Some groups find it more comfortable to start with a few questions to get conversation going. There are various ways to use questions.

- Put three or four questions in an envelope and randomly pull them out for discussion.
- Create a chart with two or three starter questions and ask the group to generate more, tapping their own personal interests and needs.
- Decide on three or four questions and divide the group by interest in the various topics. This allows for a more in-depth study.
- Make copies of the suggested questions for everyone and invite discussion without deciding where to start.

Create an Agenda

Make sure you have planned a beginning and ending time and always honor those times. Teachers are busy and knowing there will be a time to start and a time to end is important.

Stay Focused on the Topic

Plan a procedure that is transparent. You might start by saying something like, "Let's decide on a signal to use when we feel the discussion is drifting and then have everyone agree to help stay focused."

Include Everyone

Keep groups small enough so that even the quietest member is encouraged to speak. Active listening on everyone's part will help. Remember that periods of silence should be expected when people are thinking.

Share Leadership

Rotate group facilitation. Identify several "duties" for the facilitator. Examples might include a discussion format, suggesting a big idea from a chapter or group of chapters, and synthesizing or summarizing at the end. Remember that in a study group, everyone is a learner. This isn't the place for an "expert"!

Create a List of Norms

Simple expectations that are transparent often make study groups function with greater ease and increase potential for success. These can be simple and might include ways to invite a tentative member into the conversation, expectations about listening, start and stop times, and a procedure for refocusing.

Set Dates for the Next Meeting

Always leave knowing when you will meet again and who will facilitate.

Engage in Reflection

Stop from time to time to reflect on what you are learning and how you might make your group's interactions more productive.

Celebrate Learning

Make sure you take time to enjoy one another and celebrate your learning.

The following questions relate to the content in each chapter. There are suggestions and many more concepts and ideas presented in each chapter. Enjoy!

Chapter 1: Adolescent Literacy and Differentiated Instruction

1. In what ways has our definition of adolescent literacy changed over the past twenty years? How do you feel about this change in the definition? How can this changing definition be the basis for change in your teaching?

2. Several research reports have identified problems with adolescent literacy in the United States. What evidence of this have you observed? Comment on these problems or concerns relate to specifics about reading, writing, speaking, listening, viewing, and the new literacies.

3. How do you see the National Council of Teachers of English's six key practices that support adolescent literacy reflected in your school or classroom? Which of these six key practices do you believe is practiced well in your school or classroom? Which of the six key practices would you like to support better in your school or classroom?

4. Discuss how differentiated instruction can be used to support adolescent literacy. Which aspects of differentiated instruction do you feel are most relevant to adolescent learners?

Chapter 2: Adolescent Literacy and Planning for Differentiated Instruction

1. In your own words, how would you define differentiated instruction? In what ways are you and your colleagues already using instructional practices that support differentiated instruction? How did you develop your definition of differentiated instruction? Is your definition based on your own experiences, those of your teaching peers, your reading and studying, or prior workshops or professional development relating to differentiated instruction? Explain.

2. In order to differentiate instruction, teachers need to have clear goals. These clear goals begin with a basic understanding that all students must learn at high levels with teachers focusing on what is most important for all learners to know and be able to do. One model for clarifying goals is the Understanding by Design approach developed by Grant Wiggins and Jay McTighe (2005). This model includes identifying enduring understandings and essential questions for each unit. Discuss how this model or an adaptation of it can be used when planning differentiated adolescent literacy instruction.

3. What challenges to implementing differentiated instruction do you see in your school? Why do you think these challenges exist? How can these challenges be overcome?

4. Discuss why you think differentiated instruction can benefit adolescent learners.

5. Are the differentiated unit and lesson planning models provided in this chapter useful to you? How can you adopt this model to your school or district's unit and lesson planning model?

6. Discuss what type of administrative help may be needed in order to support adolescent literacy and differentiated instruction in your school. What questions and suggestions related to this topic do you have for the administrators? What is your administration's belief about differentiated instruction? What do you believe your administration would say to you about differentiated instruction?

Chapter 3: Assessment and Differentiated Instruction

1. It is sometimes said that differentiating instruction begins with assessment. How is preassessment the first step in differentiating instruction? What methods have you used to preassess learners? How have you used these methods to differentiate instruction?

2. Discuss how preassessing for interests and learning styles is as necessary as preassessing for readiness levels. What are some ways teachers can preassess students in these three areas? Categorize the methods you listed in question 1

relating to interests, learning styles, and readiness. Which category do you use most frequently? Which category of preassessing do you use the least? Why and how would you increase your use of any of the ways to preassess?

3. Differentiating assessment products can be controversial. Discuss why this can be a positive practice and consider ways it can be accomplished. Be sure to address ideas relating to equality and equity in your answer. Think of your response as an answer to parents, students, or other teachers.

4. Adolescents need to take more ownership of their own learning. Discuss how varying assessment products can help accomplish this goal while still being a reliable way for students to demonstrate learning. Consider how choice of assessments appeals to learners and how teachers can accommodate this appeal.

5. Discuss how formative assessment differs from summative assessment and why each is important. Consider how both can be used in differentiating adolescent literacy instruction. How do teachers make students part of both the formative and summative assessment processes?

6. Rick Wormeli reminds us that "fair isn't always equal" (2006b). Fair is giving each student what that person needs in order to progress. Discuss how this applies to differentiated assessment.

Chapter 4: Reading and Differentiated Instruction

1. In differentiated instruction, teachers vary the content, process, and product based on students' personal interests, readiness levels, and learning styles. Discuss how reading instruction, including the reading of fiction and nonfiction, might be differentiated.

2. Share your experiences with and views on having students read different texts within the same unit. How can a teacher select differentiated texts so that they are connected in some way? What specific texts might you use and why have you selected these texts?

3. In order for students to comprehend better what they are reading, teachers often use small-group and whole-class discussions. Socratic Seminars and

literature circles are two ways to promote true discussion. Share your experiences with these two models and discuss how they can be used to differentiate instruction.

4. Consider your own students. How might graphic novels be used to help them become more literate?

5. Share any experiences you have had with reading or teaching graphic novels.

6. Discuss your experience with and views on using electronic texts for reading in the classroom. If you have not used electronic texts, find out if other teachers you know have used them. What are their experiences? If you do not know any teachers who have used electronic texts, consult the Internet to find others who have used these texts. What do you think of their experiences?

Chapter 5: Writing and Differentiated Instruction

1. The element of choice is an important component of adolescent literacy and differentiated instruction. Share how you build choice into your writing instruction. Consider why it is important to provide adolescents choice for their writing.

2. The writing process lends itself to practices in differentiated instruction. Discuss how differentiated practices can be used at various stages of the writing process. Consider how differentiated instruction can help adolescents improve their writing.

3. Consider Lucy Calkins' model for different types of writing conferences. How can this model support adolescent literacy and differentiated instruction? Think of ways to adapt it to fit your classroom needs. Consider questions you might ask students during a writing conference. Consider how you can have adolescents take ownership of writing conferences.

4. Discuss how writing folders and portfolios can be used to differentiate instruction. Detail your own experience with folders and portfolios. Have you ever used a writing portfolio as a process collection or as a showcase? How do students learn to collect, select, and reflect?

5. Consider the benefits and the challenges of using new technology in writing instruction. How can the new technology support differentiated learning? What do you need to learn about using new technology so that you can better help your learners?

6. Discuss which of the examples presented in this chapter you use or you would consider using in your classroom and share your reasons for choosing them. Also tell about which of the examples you might have difficulty using. How might you adapt this example? What would you have to learn and do to adapt this example?

Chapter 6: Speaking, Listening, and Differentiated Instruction

1. Discuss why listening and speaking are considered essential literacy practices for adolescents. What are some of the challenges teachers face when addressing speaking and listening in the classroom?

2. Share speaking and listening assignments you have used. Discuss how these examples can be differentiated based on students' readiness levels, personal interests, and learning styles.

3. Consider ways in which technology can be used to support differentiated instruction in speaking and listening. What would you have to learn or do to use technology to support differentiated instruction in speaking and listening?

4. Share which of the examples presented in Chapter 6 you have used or plan to use and explain why.

Chapter 7: Viewing, Multimedia, and Differentiated Instruction

1. Multimedia can encompass a wide range of practices. Discuss your understanding of media literacy and its importance to adolescent literacy.

2. Discuss ways in which adolescents can become more critical viewers. What specific ways can you as their teacher help adolescents to become critical viewers?

3. Discuss ways teachers can differentiate content, process, and product when planning media literacy assignments. What are the challenges to planning and implementing such lessons?

4. Schools do not have to be high-tech to help students become more critical viewers. Share some ways teachers can instruct adolescents in critical viewing without using high-tech equipment.

Chapter 8: The New Literacies and Differentiated Instruction

1. Teachers sometimes feel left behind when it comes to developments in technology. Discuss how your faculty and administrators can support each other in this area, especially as it affects adolescent literacy.

2. Discuss what is meant by the term *new literacies*. Debate the necessity of addressing the new literacies in the English language arts classroom.

3. Podcasts, wikis, blogs, and book trailers are a few examples of new technology that can be used in classrooms to support literacy and differentiate instruction. Consider the specific examples presented in this chapter and discuss how you can use or adapt them for your own students.

4. Share your own experiences with using new technology to support adolescent literacy learning in your classroom.

5. Discuss how the new technology could be used to differentiate assignments in an English language arts classroom.

Chapter 9: Adolescent Literacy and Differentiated Instruction Beyond the Classroom

1. Discuss what role English language arts teachers can play in promoting literacy across the curriculum. What challenges do they face in doing so? Brainstorm some solutions to these challenges.

2. When considering ways to differentiate instruction to promote adolescent literacy, it is helpful to think beyond the school. Brainstorm community resources available in your area that can be used to promote adolescent literacy.

3. Middle and secondary teachers are less likely than elementary teachers to consider parents or guardians when planning lessons or activities. Discuss ways your students' parents or guardians can play a role in their adolescents' literacy development.

References

ACT (American College Testing). 2006. *Reading Between the Lines: What the ACT Reveals About College Readiness in Reading.* Iowa City, IA: ACT.

Adler, Mortimer. 1982. *The Paideia Proposal.* New York: Macmillan.

Alvermann, Donna E. 2001. "Effective Literacy Instruction for Adolescents." Executive Summary Paper of the National Reading Conference. October 30, 2001.

———. 2003. "Seeing Themselves as Capable and Engaged Readers: Adolescents and Remediated Instruction." Retrieved on November 28, 2008 from www2.learning pt.org.

———. 2007. "Multiliterate Youth in the Time of Scientific Reading Instruction." In *Adolescent Literacy: Turning Promise into Practice,* edited by Kylene Beers, Robert E. Probst, and Linda Rief. Portsmouth, NH: Heinemann.

———. 2008. "Why Bother Theorizing Adolescents' Online Literacies for Classroom Practice and Research?" *Journal of Adolescent & Adult Literacy* 52 (1): 8–19.

Armstrong, Susan, and David Warlick. 2005. "The New Literacy." *Scholastic Administrator.* March/April 2005. Retrieved on November 11, 2008 from http://content.scholastic.com.

Arnoldi, Katherine. 1998. *The Amazing "True" Story of a Teenage Single Mom.* New York: Hyperion.

Atwell, Nancie. 1998. *In the Middle.* 2d ed. Portsmouth, NH: Heinemann.

Ball, Wanda H., and Pam Brewer. 2000. *Socratic Seminar in the Block.* Larchmont, NY: Eye on Education.

Beers, Kylene, Robert E. Probst, and Linda Rief, eds. 2007. *Adolescent Literacy: Turning Promise into Practice.* Portsmouth, NH: Heinemann.

Bender, William N. 2008. *Differentiating Instruction for Students with Learning Disabilities: Best Teaching Practices for General and Special Educators.* 2d ed. Thousand Oaks, CA: Corwin Press.

Biancarosa, Gina, and Catherine E. Snow. 2006. *Reading Next: A Vision for Action and Research in Middle and High School Literacy.* Washington, DC: Alliance for Excellent Education.

Bloom, Benjamin. 1956. *Taxonomy of Educational Objectives: Handbook I: Cognitive Domain.* New York: McKay.

Brescia, William I., and Michael T. Miller. 2006. "What's It Worth? The Perceived Benefit of Instructional Blogging." *Electronic Journal for the Integration of Technology in Education* 5: 44–52.

Brookhart, Susan. 2008. *How to Give Effective Feedback to Your Students.* Alexandria, VA: ASCD.

Burke, Jim. 2000. *Reading Reminders: Tools, Tips, and Techniques.* Portsmouth, NH: Boynton/Cook.

———. 2001. *Illuminating Texts: How to Teach Students to Read the World.* Portsmouth, NH: Heinemann.

———. 2007. "Teaching English in a 'Flat' World." In *Adolescent Literacy: Turning Promise into Practice*, edited by Kylene Beers, Robert E. Probst, and Linda Rief. Portsmouth, NH: Heinemann.

Calkins, Lucy McCormick. 1994. *The Art of Teaching Writing.* Portsmouth, NH: Heinemann.

Camus, Albert. 1998. *The Stranger.* New York: Alfred Knopf, Inc.

Carter, James Bucky, ed. 2007. *Building Literacy Connections with Graphic Novels: Page by Page, Panel by Panel.* Urbana, IL: NCTE.

Cather, Willa. 1995. *My Antonia.* New York: Houghton Mifflin.

Chapman, Carolyn, and Rita King. 2003. *Differentiated Instructional Strategies for Reading in the Content Areas.* Thousand Oaks, CA: Corwin Press.

Christel, Mary T., and Scott Sullivan, eds. 2007. *Lesson Plans for Creating Media-Rich Classrooms.* Urbana, IL: NCTE.

Coiro, Julie. 2003. "Reading Comprehension on the Internet: Expanding Our Understanding of Reading Comprehension to Encompass New Literacies." *The Reading Teacher* 56 (5): 458–64.

Coiro, Julie, Michele Knobel, Colin Lankshear, and David Leu. 2008. "Central Issues in New Literacies and Research." In *Handbook of Research on New Literacies*. Mahwah, NJ: Lawrence Erlbaum.

Colombo, Michaela, and Paul D. Colombo. 2007. "Blogging to Improve Instruction in Differentiated Science Classrooms: The Need for Highly Qualified Science Teachers Who Can Differentiate Instruction for Diverse Learners Is Acute." *Phi Delta Kappan* 89 (1): 60–63.

Council of Chief State School Officers. 2007. "Adolescent Literacy Toolkit." Retrieved on January 7, 2008 from www.ccsso.org/projects/secondary_school_redesign/.

Daniels, Harvey. 2002. *Literature Circles: Voices and Choices in Book Clubs and Reading Groups*. 2d ed. Portland, ME: Stenhouse.

Daggett, Willard. 2005. "Preparing Students for Their Future." Paper presented at 2005 Model Schools Conference. Retrieved on December 1, 2008 from www.leadered .com/whitepapers.

Day, Michael. 1997. "NCTE Passes Visual Literacy Standards." *Kairos: A Journal for Teachers of Writing in Webbed Environments* 2 (1): 1. Retrieved on December 22, 2008 from http://english.ttu/Kairos/2.1/.

Dodge, Bernie. 1995. "Some Thoughts About WebQuests." Retrieved on November 16, 2008 from http://webquests.org/index.

Douglas, Karen. 2008. "Research News to Use." *Reading Today* 52 (1): 34.

Eisner, Will. 1986. *New York: The Big City*. Milwaukee, WI: Kitchen Sink Press.

Ellison, Ralph. 1968. *Invisible Man*. New York: Penguin.

Emig, Janet. 1971. *The Composing Processes of Twelfth Graders*. Urbana, IL: NCTE.

Ferdig, Richard E., and Kaye D. Trammell. 2004. "Content Delivery in the Blogosphere." *T.H.E. Journal* 31 (7): 12–15.

Fingeroth, Danny. 2008. *The Rough Guide to Graphic Novels*. New York: Rough Guides.

Fisher, Douglas B. 2007. "Adolescent Literacy: The Hottest Topic." *Journal of Adolescent & Adult Literacy* 24 (4): 12.

Fisher, Douglas, and Nancy Frey. 2007. "Altering English: Re-examining the Whole-Class Novel and Making Room for Graphic Novels and More." In *Building Literacy Connections with Graphic Novels: Page by Page, Panel by Panel*, edited by James Bucky Carter. Urbana, IL: NCTE.

Frey, Nancy, and Douglas Fisher. 2007. "Using Graphic Novels, Anime, and the Internet in an Urban High School." In *Building Literacy Connections with Graphic Novels: Page by Page, Panel by Panel*, edited by James Bucky Carter. Urbana, IL: NCTE.

Gardner, Howard. 1983. *Frames of Mind: The Theory of Multiple Intelligences*. New York: Basic Books.

————. 1993. *Multiple Intelligences: The Theory in Practice.* New York: Basic Books.

Golden, John. 2001. *Reading in the Dark: Using Film as a Tool in the English Classroom.* Urbana, IL: NCTE.

Goodyear, Dyna. 2008. "Letter from Japan; I Love Novels." *The New Yorker* December 22 and 29, 62–68.

Graham, Steven, and Delores Perin. 2007. *Writing Next: Effective Strategies to Improve Writing Instruction of Adolescents in Middle and High Schools, A Report to Carnegie Corporation of New York.* Washington, DC: Alliance for Excellent Education.

Gregory, Gayle H., and Carolyn Chapman. 2003. *Differentiated Instructional Strategies for Reading in the Content Areas.* Thousand Oaks, CA: Corwin Press.

Harvey, Stephanie, and Anne Goudvis. 2007. *Strategies That Work: Teaching Comprehension for Understanding and Engagement.* 2d ed. Portland, ME: Stenhouse.

Henning, Jeffrey. 2003. "The Blogging Iceberg: Of 4.12 Million Hosted Weblogs, Most Little Seen, Quickly Abandoned." Perseus Development Corporation. Retrieved on November 20, 2008 from www.perseus.com/blogsurvey/thebloggingiceberg.html.

Hess, Rebekah. 2008. "Podcasting in the English Classroom." Retrieved on November 5, 2008 from http://cnx.org/content/m18043/latest.

Hiaasen, Carl. 2007. *Hoot.* New York: Alfred Knopf.

Huffaker, David. 2004. "The Educated Blogger: Using Weblogs to Promote Literacy in the Classroom." *First Monday.* Retrieved on November 9, 2008 from www.first monday.org.

Hurston, Zora Neale. 1999. *Their Eyes Were Watching God.* New York: Harper Collins.

International Reading Association. 2001. *Integrating Literacy and Technology into the Curriculum: A Position Statement.* Newark, DE: IRA.

Irvin, Judith L., Julie Meltzer, and Melinda S. Dukes. 2007. *Taking Action on Adolescent Literacy: An Implementation Guide for School Leaders.* Alexandria, VA: ASCD.

Kajder, Sara. 2003. *The Tech-Savvy English Classroom.* Portland, ME: Stenhouse.

————. 2004. "Plugging In: What Technology Brings to the English Language Arts Classroom." *Voices from the Middle* 11 (3): 6–9.

————. 2006. *Bringing the Outside In: Visual Ways to Engage Student Readers.* Portland, ME: Stenhouse.

————. 2007. "Unleashing the Potential with Emerging Technologies." In *Adolescent Literacy: Promise into Practice,* edited by Kylene Beers, Robert E. Probst, and Linda Rief, 213–39. Portsmouth, NH: Heinemann.

Kelly, Kevin. 2008. "Becoming Screen Literate." *New York Times Sunday Magazine* November 23: 48–57.

King-Shaver, Barbara. 2005. *When Text Meets Text: Helping High School Readers Make Connections in Literature.* Portsmouth, NH: Heinemann.

King-Shaver, Barbara, and Alyce Hunter. 2003. *Differentiated Instruction in the English Classroom: Content, Process, Product, and Assessment*. Portsmouth, NH: Heinemann.

Lesesne, Teri S. 2007. "Of Time, Teens, and Books." In *Adolescent Literacy: Turning Promise into Practice*, edited by Kylene Beers, Robert E. Probst, and Linda Rief, 61–79. Portsmouth, NH: Heinemann.

Leu, Donald. 2008. "The New Literacies of Online Reading Comprehension: Preparing All Students for Their Reading Futures." Retrieved on October 18, 2008 from www.newliteracies.uconn.edu.

Leu, Donald J., Jr., Charles K. Kinzer, Julie L. Coiro, and Dana W. Cammack. 2004. "Toward a Theory of New Literacies Emerging from the Internet and Other Information and Communication Technologies." In *Theoretical Models and Processes of Reading*, 5th ed., edited by Robert B. Ruddell and Norman J. Unrau. Newark, DE: IRA.

Levine, Judith L., Julie Meltzer, and Melinda Dukes. 2007. *Taking Action on Adolescent Literacy: An Implementation Plan for School Leaders*. Alexandria, VA: ASCD.

March, Tom. 2004. "The Learning Power of WebQuests." *Educational Leadership* 61 (4): 42–46.

Marshall, Kim. 2008. "Interim Assessment: A User's Guide." *Phi Delta Kappan* 90 (1): 64–68.

Miller, Arthur. 2000. "Are You Now or Were You Ever?" Retrieved on December 1, 2008 from http://www.guardian.co.uk/books/2000/jun/17/history.society.

Moffett, James, and Betty Jane Wagner. 1992. *Student-Centered Language Arts Curriculum K–12*. 4th ed. Portsmouth, NH: Boynton/Cook & Heinemann.

National Assessment of Educational Progress (NAEP). 2007. "The Nation's Report Card 2007." NAEP Report. Retrieved on December 28, 2008 from http://nationsreport card.gov.

National Association of Secondary School Principals. 2005. *Creating a Culture of Literacy: A Guide for Middle and High School Principals*. Reston, VA: NASSP.

National Commission on Writing. 2006. *The Neglected "R": The Need for a Writing Revolution*. New York: The College Board.

National Council of Teachers of English. 1996. "Resolution on Viewing and Visually Representing as Forms of Literacy." Retrieved on December 28, 2008 from www.ncte.org/positions/statements.

———. 2004. "A Call for Action: What We Know About Adolescent Literacy and Ways to Support Teachers in Meeting Students' Needs." May 2004. NCTE guideline prepared by the NCTE Executive Committee. Retrieved on January 26, 2008 from www.ncte.org.

———. 2006. "Principles of Adolescent Literacy Reform: A Policy Research Brief." April 2006. Urbana, IL: NCTE. Retrieved on November 28, 2008 from www.reading.org/positionstatement.

———. 2007. "Adolescent Literacy: A Policy Research Brief." September 2007. Retrieved on January 26, 2008 from www.ncte.org.

———. 2008a. "Reading and Writing Differently." James R. Squire Office of Policy Research Report. *The Council Chronicle* 18 (2): 15–129.

———. 2008b. *Writing Now: A Policy Research Brief.* September 2008. Urbana, IL: NCTE.

National Council of Teachers of English and International Reading Association. 1996. *Standards for the English Language Arts.* Urbana, IL and Newark, DE: NCTE/IRA.

Nunley, Kathie F. 2006. *Differentiating the High School Classroom: Solution Strategies for 18 Common Obstacles.* Thousand Oaks, CA: Corwin Press.

O'Brien, David, and Cassandra Barber. 2008. "Digital Literacies Go to School: Potholes and Possibilities." *Journal of Adolescent & Adult Literacy* 52 (1): 66–68.

Ogle, Donna. 1986. "K.W.L.: A Teaching Method That Develops Actual Reading of Expository Text." *The Reading Teacher* 39: 563–70.

Onishi, Norimitsu. 2008. "Sore Thumbs in Japan as Best Sellers Go Cellular." *The New York Times*, January 20, International Section, p. 1ff.

Oravec, JoAnn. 2002. "Bookmarking the World: Weblog Applications in Education." *Journal of Adolescent & Adult Literacy* 45 (7): 616–21.

Popham, W. James. 2003. *Test Better, Teach Better: The Instructional Role of Assessment.* Alexandria, VA: ASCD.

———. 2008. *Transformative Assessment.* Alexandria, VA: ASCD.

Probst, Robert E. 2001. *Response & Analysis: Teaching Literature in the Secondary School.* 2d ed. Portsmouth, NH: Heinemann.

———. 2007. "Tom Sawyer, Teaching and Talking." In *Adolescent Literacy: Turning Promise into Practice*, edited by Kylene Beers, Robert E. Probst, and Linda Rief, 43–59. Portsmouth, NH: Heinemann.

Raphael, Taffy, and P. David Pearson. 1982. *The Effect of Metacognitive Awareness Training on Children's Question Answering Behavior.* Technical Report No. 238. Urbana, IL: Center for the Study of Reading.

Richardson, Will. 2006. *Blogs, Wikis, Podcasts and Other Powerful Tools for Today's Classrooms.* Thousand Oaks, CA: Corwin Press.

Routman, Regie. 1991. *Invitations: Changing as Teachers and Learners, K–12.* Toronto: Irwin.

Santa, Carol Minnick. 1988. *Content Reading Including Study Systems.* Dubuque, IA: Kendall/ Hunt.

Satrapi, Marjane. 2003. *Persepolis*. New York: Pantheon.

Schmoker, Michael. 2006. *Results Now*. Alexandria, VA: ASCD.

Schraffenberger, J. D. 2007. "Visualizing Beowulf: Old English Gets Graphic." In *Building Literacy Connections with Graphic Novels: Page by Page, Panel by Panel*, edited by James Bucky Carter. Urbana, IL: NCTE.

Schwartz, Gretchen. 2002. "Graphic Novels for Multiple Literacies." *Journal of Adolescent & Adult Literacy* 46: 262–65.

Shanklin, Nancy. 2008. "Webquests: A Literacy/Technology Practice That Fosters Adolescent's Curiosity." *Voices from the Middle* 16 (1): 48–50.

Shuster, Kate. 2006. "Debate: It's Misunderstood." Retrieved on December 20, 2008 from www.middleschooldebate.com.

Shuster, Kate, and John Meany. 2005. *Speak Out! Debate and Public Speaking in the Middle Grades*. New York: International Debate Education Association.

Smith, Frank. 1978. *Understanding Reading: A Psycholinguistic Analysis of Reading and Learning to Read*. New York: Holt, Rinehart and Winston.

Smith, Jeff. 2004. *Bone*. Columbus, OH: Cartoon Books.

Smith, Michael W., and Jeffrey D. Wilhelm. 2002. *Reading Don't Fix No Chevys: Literacy in the Lives of Young Men*. Portsmouth, NH: Heinemann.

Spiegelman, Art. 1986. *Maus I: A Survivor's Tale*. New York: Pantheon.

———. 1991. *Maus II: A Survivor's Tale*. New York: Pantheon.

Stevens, Lisa Patel, and Thomas W. Bean. 2007. *Critical Literacy: Context, Research, and Practice in the K–12 Classroom*. Thousand Oaks, CA: Sage.

Strickland, Kathleen, and James Strickland. 2002. *Engaged in Learning: Teaching English, 6–12*. Portsmouth, NH: Heinemann.

Sullivan, Scott. 2007. "Introduction: Media Literacy: Finding a Foothold in the English Classroom." In *Lesson Plans for Creating Media-Rich Classrooms*, edited by Mary T. Christel and Scott Sullivan. Urbana, IL: NCTE.

Teasley, Alan B., and Ann Wilder. 1994. "Teaching Visual Literacy: 50 Great Young Adult Films." *The ALAN Review* 21 (3): 18–23.

Thibault, Melissa, and David Walbert. 2003. "Reading Images: An Introduction to Visual Literacy." LEARN NC. Retrieved on October 28, 2008 from http://learnnc .org/lp/pages/675?style=print.

Tomlinson, Carol Ann. 1999. *The Differentiated Classroom: Responding to the Needs of All Learners*. Alexandria, VA: ASCD.

———. 2001 "Leadership for Differentiated Instruction." Retrieved on November 26, 2008 from www.aasa.org/publications/sa/1999_10/tomlinson.html.

———. 2003. *Fulfilling the Promise of a Differentiated Classroom: Strategies & Tools for Responsive Teaching*. Alexandria, VA: ASCD.

———. 2008. "The Goals of Differentiation." *Educational Leadership* 66 (3): 26–30.

Tomlinson, Carol Ann, and Jay McTighe. 2006. *Integrating Differentiated Instruction & Understanding by Design.* Alexandria, VA: ASCD.

Tovani, Cris. 2004a. *Do I Really Have to Teach Reading?* Portland, ME: Stenhouse.

———. 2004b. *I Read It, But I Don't Get It: Comprehension Skills of Adolescent Readers.* Portland, ME: Stenhouse.

Tukey, L. 2002. "Differentiation." *Educational Leadership* 84 (1): 63.

"Using Comics and Graphic Novels in the Classroom." 2005, September. *The Council Chronicle.* Retrieved on November 11, 2008 from www.ncte.org.

Watts, Pailliotet, et al. 2000. "Intermediality: Bridge to Critical Media Literacy." *The Reading Teacher* 54: 208–19.

Wells, Gordon. 1999. *Dialogue Inquiry: Towards a Sociocultural Practice and Theory of Education.* Cambridge: Cambridge University Press.

———. 2003. "Children Talk Their Way into Literacy." Originally published in J. R. Garcia, ed. *Ensenar a Escribir sin Prisas . . . Pero con Sentido.* Sevilla, Spain: Publicaciones M.C.E.P. Retrieved on December 24, 2008 from http://people.ucsc.edu/~gwells.files/papers/talk-literacy.pdf.

"What Is Critical Viewing?" Retrieved November 17, 2008 from www.medialit.org/reading_room/article340.html.

Wiggins, Grant. 2006. "Healthier Testing Made Easy: The Idea of Authentic Assessment." *Edutopia* April 2006.

Wiggins, Grant, and Jay McTighe. 2005. *Understanding by Design.* Alexandria, VA: ASCD.

Williams, Jeremy B., and Joanne Jacobs. 2004. "Exploring the Use of Blogs as Learning Spaces in the Higher Education Sector." *Australian Journal of Educational Technology* 20 (2): 232–47.

Williams, Scott. 2007. "Turning Text into Movie Trailers." In *Lesson Plans for Creating Media-Rich Classrooms,* edited by Mary T. Christel and Scott Sullivan. Urbana, IL: NCTE.

Witherell, Nancy L., and Mary C. McMackin. 2002. *Graphic Organizers and Activities for Differentiating Instruction in Reading.* New York: Scholastic Professional Books.

Wormeli, Rick. 2006a. "Differentiating for Tweens." *Educational Leadership* 63 (2): 14–19.

———. 2006b. *Fair Isn't Always Equal: Assessing & Grading in the Differentiated Classroom.* Portland, ME: Stenhouse.

Yancey, Kathleen Blake. 2008. "Planning for a Future Very Different from Our Own." *The Council Chronicle* September: 28–29.

Yang, Gene. 2008. "Graphic Novels in the Classroom." *Language Arts* 85 (3): 185–92.

Index